Bad News for Race Hustlers

Bad News for Race Hustlers

Larry Elder

Creators Publishing
Hermosa Beach, CA

Bad News for Race Hustlers
Copyright © 2018 Laurence A. Elder

Cover art by Peter Kaminski

CREATORS PUBLISHING
737 3rd St
Hermosa Beach, CA 90254
310-337-7003

ISBN (print): 978-1-945630-91-0
ISBN (ebook): 978-1-945630-90-3

First Edition
Printed in the United States of America
1 3 5 7 9 10 8 6 4 2

Contents

A Note From the Publisher

Since 1987, Creators has syndicated many of your favorite columns to newspapers. In this digital age, we are bringing collections of those columns to your fingertips. This will allow you to read and reread your favorite columnists, with your own personal digital archive of their work.

Creators Publishing

'Repeal and Replace' Obamacare — With the Free Market

January 5, 2017

One of President-elect Donald Trump's major campaign promises is to "repeal and replace" Obamacare.

Vice President Joe Biden recently dared him to do so. Biden knows that 20 million Americans have health insurance that didn't before Obamacare, and they represent 20 million stories on CNN, MSNBC and The New York Times — in the entire "health care is a right" crowd — when and if Trump follows through.

Sure, despite President Barack Obama's promises to the contrary, some people lost their health care coverage and some people lost their doctors. And no, the average family did not save $2,500 per year as Obama insisted would be the case. And yes, health insurance premiums, copays and deductibles are going up even though Obama promised that his plan would "bend the cost curve" down.

All that matters to the anti-Trump media is that there is now an entire class of people to exert pressure against the repeal of Obamacare. Many Republicans say they want to keep "the good parts of Obamacare," specifically the prohibition against denying insurance based on a pre-existing condition and forcing insurance carriers to keep a "child" on his or her parents' policy until the child is 26. Republicans promised to not only repeal but to "replace" Obamacare. How can they do this — and replace it with what?

Republicans, despite their unanimous opposition against Obamacare, bought into at least two premises that its proponents argued. The first is that health care is a right — or, if not a right, at least something whose costs the federal government should reduce. The second is that, having made the decision to intervene in health care, the federal government possesses the knowledge, wisdom and judgment to reduce its costs to make it "affordable." The feds, promised Obamacare advocates, can even make health care affordable without reducing quality.

For Obamacare to "work," it is particularly important for young people to "buy in," because while they are forced to *spend* on health care insurance they are unlikely to *consume* health care services. Obamacare transfers money from the pockets of young people (with a net worth smaller than that of seniors, by the way) into the pockets of older, health care consuming Americans.

If the goal were truly to make health care more affordable, Obamacare would be as laughably wrongheaded as other Obama boondoggles like "cash for caulkers" or "cash for clunkers." No, the real goal is taxpayer-paid health care. Both ex-DNC chair Howard Dean and ex-Senate leader Harry Reid said so.

To reduce costs in health care, or, for that matter, in *any* commodity, is to unleash the free market. Health care is particularly shackled by restrictions and regulations too numerous to mention. Here is just one example.

In the biographical movie "Hacksaw Ridge," a World War II medic, Private Desmond Doss, a pacifist, refused to carry a rifle. In the midst of the carnage, during the Battle of Okinawa, Doss carried wounded soldiers and rappelled them down a cliff face to safety then treated them alongside the medics. He was awarded a Medal of Honor for saving scores of lives.

If, however, after the war, Pvt. Doss had opened an office with a shingle saying "Doss' trauma unit," authorities would have thrown him in jail for practicing medicine without a license. His skills were good enough for the soldiers on the battlefield, but not good enough for civilians when Doss returned stateside.

On a question-and-answer website, this question was recently posed: How do Marines feel about Navy corpsmen?

Here are some of the responses: "Personal experience — I had my middle finger sewn back on by an E-5 corpsman. When a real doctor first saw it, he shouted, 'Who did this?!' I asked why and the

Doc said that it was the best he had ever seen. I have full use and feeling in that finger and that was 40 years ago."

"Personal experience — I was shot in the leg. An E-4 corpsman, assisted by an E-5, treated me. No doctor could have done any better than they did."

"History: Beginning in WWII, most ships the size of destroyers and smaller had enlisted men — corpsmen — as their only medical expert. Usually it was a Chief Petty Officer, but often was an E-6 and some had only an E-5.

"Then, as now, they did everything — surgery included. In WWII and every war since then, U.S. soldiers have had a higher survival rate than any other country's military (enemy or allies) and most of that medical triage and vital systems treatment was by enlisted corpsmen.

"Outside the service, enlisted corpsmen are by far the preferable hire for civilian EMT and rescue jobs."

If Congressional Republicans were serious about making health care affordable, they should sell the voters on the free market. Where's the slogan for that?

Living Wage Is as Wrongheaded as the Minimum Wage

January 12, 2017

What future will America have when so many of her citizens lack the ability to engage in critical thinking, refuse to connect the dots, and fail to use common sense?

This unwillingness to think clearly is no better demonstrated than by the continued support for the minimum wage. After all the studies and the near-unanimous opinion of economists — and even after the negative real-world effect of the minimum wage — it still remains popular.

Why?

Sadly, most people are simply unaware of the argument against the minimum wage. They just don't know about the vast body of research that shows the harm.

American Federation of Teachers President Randi Weingarten recently called for a "living wage." In a speech to the National Press Club, Weingarten said, "We need to fight for a living wage, for retirement security, for affordable and accessible health care and college, and for universal pre-K, to name a few."

Maybe the problem is that liberals, like Weingarten, simply pay no attention to what conservatives say. So let's use liberals. Two of the most well-known liberal economists have criticized the minimum wage and its twin, the living wage.

Jonathan Gruber, the architect of Massachusetts' Romneycare and co-architect of Obamacare, said in 2011: "Let's say the government rolled in and set a minimum wage. ... Workers want to supply more hours than firms want to hire. ... You end up with excess supply. And we call that excess supply 'unemployment.'" Gruber discussed the pressure that raising minimum wage puts on employers to turn to automation: "We have a downward-sloping demand curve, and why is it downward sloping? Because the higher the wage, the fewer workers the firm wants to hire. It would rather use machines instead."

Gruber once argued against paid leave, as well. Employers, he said, will simply reduce wages so that the overall compensation cost to employers is the same, giving the worker no net benefit. In 1994 Gruber wrote: "I study several state and federal mandates which stipulated that childbirth be covered comprehensively in health insurance plans, raising the relative cost of insuring women of childbearing age. I find substantial shifting of the costs of these mandates to the wages of the targeted group." In other words, if an employer is forced to pay for family leave, the employer will simply reduce the employee's wages to offset the cost.

The New York Times left-wing columnist and economist Paul Krugman also made the case against the minimum wage. In 1998, Krugman reviewed a book that supported the living wage, titled "The Living Wage: Building a Fair Economy." Krugman opposed it: "The living wage movement is simply a move to raise minimum wages through local action. So what are the effects of increasing minimum wages? Any Econ 101 student can tell you the answer: The higher wage reduces the quantity of labor demanded, and hence leads to unemployment."

Krugman even dismissed a widely cited study that purports to show the positive effect of minimum wages: "Indeed, much-cited studies by two well-regarded labor economists, David Card and Alan Krueger, find that where there have been more or less controlled experiments, for example when New Jersey raised minimum wages but Pennsylvania did not, the effects of the increase on employment have been negligible or even positive. Exactly what to make of this result is a source of great dispute. Card and Krueger offered some complex theoretical rationales, but most of their colleagues are unconvinced; the centrist view is probably that minimum wages 'do,' in fact, reduce employment. ..."

"In short, what the living wage is really about is not living standards, or even economics, but morality. Its advocates are basically opposed to the idea that wages are a market price - determined by supply and demand, the same as the price of apples or coal."

Minimum- and living-wage proponents also support equal pay for men and women. By doing so they make inconsistent arguments. On the one hand, employers are so cheap and greedy that they would pay virtually nothing for labor if the government did not force their hand.

On the other hand, the same greedy employers are happily overpaying men who, according to the equal-wage activists, are being paid more than women for doing the exact same work. Why a greedy employer would both underpay and overpay at the same time is never explained.

Trump 'Disrespects' the Intel Community? What About Obama's Iraq Bug-Out?

January 19, 2017

President Barack Obama and his team *still* engage in a hissy fit over Donald Trump's questioning Obama's place of birth. To even raise the issue is to "otherwise" the first black President. In short, they argue, it is racist. But to claim that Vladimir Putin put Trump in the White House is nothing more than an obvious observation, right? When the Supreme Court ruled in favor of George W. Bush in 2000, a number of disgruntled Democrats referred to him as "President Select."

Now President-elect Trump is being hammered over his refusal to accept the intelligence community's consensus about Russia's alleged role in the election. All of the intel agencies maintain that the Russian government attempted to influence our election, and that Russia preferred Trump over Hillary Clinton.

From the outset, Trump doubted both the argument that Russia hacked the Democratic National Committee and that the release of damaging emails was designed to give him an advantage over his rival. Trump, at least before his recent national security briefing, argued that the hacking could've been done by a number of actors, including China and other state and non-state entities. Trump's reluctance to accept the apparent unanimous opinion of our intel agencies probably has more to do with his rejection of the narrative that but for Russia he would not be president.

Russian President Vladimir Putin did not tell Clinton to put a private server in her basement in Chappaqua. Putin did not tell Clinton to delete 30,000 emails while arguing that they were not work related. He did not tell her to destroy evidence that was under subpoena. He did not tell her to falsely assert that she never sent or received classified information, or to falsely claim that she never sent or received information that was stamped classified.

Putin did not tell the DNC to ridicule the name of a black woman or to condescendingly suggest that the way to get Hispanic votes was through "brand loyalty" and "stories" because, after all, "Hispanics are the most responsive to 'story telling.' Brands need to 'speak with us.'" Nor did Putin get Hillary Clinton campaign Chairman John Podesta to agree that the Iran deal is "the greatest appeasement since Chamberlain gave Czechoslovakia to Hitler."

But the "Trump doesn't respect the intel community" argument raises another issue. Why doesn't Obama get the same criticism for rejecting his national security and intelligence team's advice on Iraq?

As a candidate, Obama called the Iraq War "dumb." He vowed to withdraw the troops and reposition them in Afghanistan — the good war. As President, this is exactly what he did.

But he did so against the unanimous advice of the major national security voices in his administration.

Then-Secretary of State Hillary Clinton urged him to keep a stay-behind force. So did his secretary of Defense, the head of the CIA, the Joint Chiefs of Staff, the United States ambassador to Iraq and his national security adviser.

Army Gen. Ray Odierno, former member of the Joint Chiefs of Staff, said shorty after his retirement that had there been a stabilizing force in Iraq, ISIS could've been dealt with: "I go back to the work we did in 2007 (through) 2010, and we got into a place that was really good. Violence was low, the economy was growing, politics looked like it was heading in the right direction. ... We thought we had it going exactly in the right direction, but now we watch it fall apart. It's frustrating that it's falling apart. ... I think, maybe, if we had stayed a little bit more engaged, I think maybe it might have prevented it."

Think about it. Obama, with barely two years of experience in the Senate, and no foreign-policy experience, rejected the unanimous advice of his mission security team. He pulled completely out of Iraq, a decision that aided and abetted the rise of ISIS.

Trump gets hammered for ignoring the unanimous opinion of the intelligence community; Obama makes one of the most consequential decisions by completely ignoring their advice. And, as usual, Obama gets a pass.

Under Republican President Trump, the Media Rediscovers Its Purpose

January 26, 2017

Only hours into his new job, White House press secretary Sean Spicer attacked the media for what he called "dishonesty" and "deliberately false reporting." He specifically challenged the reporting that said President Donald Trump's inauguration had a smaller audience than the inaugurations of President Barack Obama and that Trump removed the bust of Martin Luther King Jr. from the Oval Office.

Many in the media counterattacked and accused Spicer of peddling "falsehoods," one even nicknaming him "Baghdad Sean," likening him to Saddam Hussein's information minister, "Baghdad Bob," who blithely assured Iraqis that all was well as that country fell to U.S. troops in 2003. Left-wing pundits on cable said things like, "How do you cover an administration that has such a casual relationship with the truth?"

The answer is quite simple. Just do as you did when President Obama peddled falsehood after falsehood for the last eight years.

Obama, for example, said many times that he was "most proud" of "saving the American economy." He even made this assertion during press conferences, when reporters could have challenged him. Last year, he expanded his "most proud" resume to include "saving the world economy from a great depression."

Did the media inform the public that recoveries always follow recessions, and that, had Obama done nothing, history shows the recovery would have been more robust than what we experienced under Obama? The average recovery, for the last eight recessions dating back to 1960, is 3.9 percent inflation-adjusted annual GDP growth. Obama's recovery, which began after the recession ended in June 2009, averaged 2.1 percent. President Ronald Reagan's averaged 4.8 percent, which translates, according to the Heritage Foundation's Stephen Moore when he calculated it in 2015, into a per-family average of $20,000 more in income. An increase of 1 percent growth in GDP brings roughly 1 million more jobs. So had Obama done nothing, history suggests there would have been 13 million more jobs than were created during Obama's recovery.

When Obama first said, "If you like your doctor, you can keep your doctor," one could argue that he did not deceive, since the plan was not fully fleshed out. But after the administration began writing the regulations, it soon became clear that one could not keep his or her doctor or plan. Still Obama continued to say, "If you like your doctor, you can keep your doctor." Did a suddenly aggressive media hold Obama accountable for knowingly pushing a falsehood?

Obama got a pass for pulling all the troops out of Iraq. Not only did he do so against the advice of his entire national security team; he then pushed the whopper that his predecessor, President George W. Bush, tied his hands. Incredibly, Obama, who reneged on defense deals negotiated between Bush and Poland and the Czech Republic, claimed that Bush's status of forces agreement *required* him to pull completely out of Iraq — and by the Bush-set timetable. No, it did not. Bush's deal envisioned that his successor would negotiate a stay-behind force, something that Obama clearly could have done if he so chose.

Obama also sold Obamacare on a big falsehood that the media never seemed particularly exercised about. On a number of occasions, he claimed that when his mother was dying of cancer her insurance carrier had to be browbeaten into paying her doctor and medical bills. False. All her hospital, medical and doctor bills were paid. The only dispute between Obama's mother and an insurance carrier was over a disability policy, which she had taken out *after* having been diagnosed with cancer. Such a policy doesn't cover a disability caused by a pre-existing condition, and the insurance carrier properly and successfully challenged the claim.

After the 2000 election, The Wall Street Journal's OpinionJournal.com introduced what it called the "Homelessness Rediscovery Watch," to point out that with a Republican in the White House the media would print more stories about the homeless. Now that a Republican — especially one as disliked Donald Trump — is in the White House, the media rediscovers its aggressiveness and zeal to "hold the President accountable." The New York Times even used the word "lie" in a headline about Trump's assertion that he would have won the popular vote but for millions who voted illegally.

Welcome back, media. We missed you.

ESPN Tennis Analyst Sacked Over Bogus Charge of Racism

February 2, 2017

Doug Adler does tennis commentary for ESPN. Strike that. Doug Adler *used* to do tennis commentary for ESPN. After several years working matches for the sports channel, the former tennis pro was advised that his services would no longer be necessary.

Full disclosure. I've known Adler for 20 years. Before two back surgeries and a shoulder surgery put my tennis-playing days out to pasture, I hit balls with him at a neighborhood club. More precisely, he would hit the ball to me, and I would attempt to return it. At the club, Adler was well-liked. If there were a bad word said about him, I never heard it.

So what happened?

While doing commentary for a Venus Williams match against Stefanie Voegele in the recent Australian Open tennis tournament, Adler made the following comment about Williams' strategy following her opponent's missed first serves: "(Voegele) misses a first serve and Venus is all over her. You'll see Venus move in and put the guerilla effect on. Charging."

For 36 hours, Adler said, "Nothing happened."

Then ESPN informed him, "There is a problem." Why, he was asked, did he refer to Venus Williams, a black woman, as a "gorilla"? Adler was told that, among other complaints, a tennis writer for The New York Times, Ben Rothenberg, tweeted: "This is some appalling stuff. Horrifying that the Williams sisters remain subjected to it still in 2017." He also tweeted: "And this is why it's so problematic. Innocent mistake or not, there has to be way, way more awareness and sensitivity."

ESPN issued this statement: "During an Australian Open stream on ESPN3, Doug Adler should have been more careful in his word selection. He apologized and we have removed him from his remaining assignments."

Adler insists that he did not say "gorilla." He says that he said "guerrilla," a word with no racial connotation. Other tennis commentators, he notes, use the word "guerrilla" to describe aggressive, attacking-style play.

An April 2, 2012, Sports Illustrated story had the following headline: "Daily Bagel: Agnieszka Radwanska Playing 'Guerrilla Tennis.'" The headline referred to a March 31, 2012, profile and interview of Radwanska by tennis writer Peter Bodo on Tennis.com, which included: "The adjectives that come to mind to describe Radwanska are: Implacable; remote; unflappable; leisurely; languid; measured. ... Hers is a game of the insurgent. It's *guerrilla* (emphasis added) tennis — especially against taller, more powerful, more physical rivals."

In an ESPN.com article dated Jan. 26, 2013, Bodo wrote about a five-set match between Roger Federer and Andy Murray: "Against Federer, Murray confirmed that his new, more aggressive game can bear up under world-class stress. The 25-year-old Scot dictated the tone and pace of that match. He forced his 31-year-old rival, the all-time singles Grand Slam champion, to fight a bitter *guerrilla* (emphasis added) war."

Despite believing that he did nothing wrong, Adler apologized that he "simply and inadvertently chose the wrong word to describe her play." The apology did not save his relationship with ESPN, and he soon lost another tennis commentary job with a different channel due to the Williams "controversy."

Williams, by the way, was asked during the tournament about Adler's comment. She said she was aware of the matter, but wanted to concentrate on winning and declined to give an opinion. Who knows whether she said something behind the scenes.

This is similar to what happened years ago to a former aide to the newly elected black mayor of Washington, D.C. David Howard, a white man, used the word "niggardly" in a conversation about funding with two of his staffers. After seeing their reaction to the word, Howard immediately apologized to his entire three-person staff, two of whom were black. But a rumor shot around City Hall that Howard used a "racial slur." Niggardly, of course, means stingy or miserly, and has nothing to do with race. No matter; the controversy cause the aide to resign.

Adler says that several fellow tennis commentators privately contacted him, and agreed that he said nothing wrong. None of these commentators, however, has spoken out publicly on Adler's behalf.

ESPN has standards. One of its football commentators, Ray Lewis, once pled guilty to obstruction of justice in a murder case. Director Spike Lee has worked with ESPN, despite the fact that we once said he disliked interracial couples: "I give interracial couples a look. Daggers. They get uncomfortable when they see me on the street."

Adler's plight once again illustrates that America has zero tolerance for anti-black racism. John O'Sullivan, former editor of National Review, once wrote: "White racism does exist, but its social power is weak and the social power arrayed against it overwhelming."

But this was not a case of "white racism" — it was a case of racial hysteria.

Audi and Snoop Dogg During the Super Bowl

February 9, 2017

The exciting recent Super Bowl meant that fans paid more attention to the game than to the commercials. But there were some doozies, including the 84 Lumber commercial that sympathetically depicted a Latina mother and her young daughter trying to cross the border and enter America, only to encounter a foreboding wall. Hint, hint: President Trump wants to build a wall on the southern border. But at least two other commercials stood out.

An Audi commercial highlighted the alleged problem of women receiving unequal pay. A male voice says: "What do I tell my daughter? Do I tell her that her grandpa is worth more than her grandma? That her dad is worth more than her mom? Do I tell her that despite her education, her drive, her skills, her intelligence, she will automatically be valued as less than every man she ever meets?" Audi also tweeted: "Women are still paid 21 percent less than men."

It is a lie that women make less money than men for the same work. How do we know? Audi admits it. Turns out, Audi pays its female employees less than its male employees. In response to this inconvenient fact, Audi said: "When we account for all the various factors that go into pay, women at Audi are on par with their male counterparts." Of Audi's six-person management board, there is not a single female. Of Audi's American top-management staff of 14, two are women.

Then there was the T-Mobile spot featuring rapper Snoop Dogg and entrepreneur/domestic-goddess Martha Stewart. Only weeks earlier, Snoop Dogg — using language you definitely wouldn't hear in a Super Bowl ad — threatened to ridicule any black person who agreed to perform at President Donald Trump's inauguration. To people like Snoop Dogg, blacks who support Trump, like Dr. Ben Carson, Trump's pick for secretary of the Department of Housing and Urban Development, are sellouts. A black writer for The Daily Beast slammed Carson in a piece titled: "Ben Carson Was a Role Model for Black Teens Until He Sold Out to the Right."

Sold out? What about Snoop Dogg?

Most rap music is purchased by white teens living in the suburbs. In 2004, Mediamark Research estimated the percentage of rap bought by whites at 60 percent. If most of the buyers of rap are white, doesn't this mean rappers like Snoop are performing for whites? Doesn't this make him every bit the "sellout" that he considers Carson?

In Snoop Dogg's music, he routinely uses derogatory words to describe women. He wrote and starred in a self-titled X-rated porn film. He romanticizes drugs. Where are the angry feminists when we need them? Meanwhile, Republican Carson, raised in poverty by a single mom, who talks about the importance of family, education and hard work, is to be demeaned and dismissed as an Uncle Tom.

A common theme of rap is racial oppression and victimization in America, a country that supposedly persecuted blacks. In the case of Snoop Dogg, whose real name is Calvin Broadus, it's a rather charmed persecution. In 1996, Broadus and a bodyguard stood trial for murder. The victim was a reputed gang member who also happened to be black.

A Los Angeles jury acquitted both defendants of murder but could not reach a verdict as to whether the two had committed voluntary manslaughter and whether Broadus had committed conspiracy after the fact by allegedly attempting to destroy evidence. As to the manslaughter charge, the jury foreman said the last vote was 9-3 but refused to say whether the vote was 9-3 in favor of acquittal or conviction. So, at the very least, three jurors believed the future pitchman for products like T-Mobile and Chrysler had committed manslaughter. A $25 million wrongful death lawsuit filed by the victim's family was settled "amicably."

Stewart, it should be noted, was convicted of felony charges of conspiracy, obstruction of an agency proceeding and making false statements to federal investigators. She lied to the FBI in connection with an insider-trading investigation and served five months in a federal prison.

T-Mobile clearly believes in second chances.

As to the Super Bowl, Lady Gaga gave a patriotic halftime performance mostly devoid of politics. During the playing of the national anthem, no one took a knee. The balls appeared to be properly inflated. The New England Patriots, down 25 points, overcame the largest deficit in Super Bowl history to win in the final play of the first-ever Super Bowl overtime game. It was enough to make one forget about the annoying commercials. Almost.

John F. Kennedy: What Would He Think of His Party?

February 16, 2017

President Ronald Reagan said: "I didn't leave the Democratic Party. The party left me." Actor and former president of the National Rifle Association Charlton Heston, who called himself a "Kennedy Democrat," switched to the Republican Party after the 1960s.

On racial preferences, JFK, in 1963, said he opposed them: "I don't think that is the generally held view, at least as I understand it, of the Negro community, that there is some compensation due for the lost years, particularly in the field of education. What I think they would like is to see their children well-educated so that they could hold jobs and have their children accepted and have themselves accepted as equal members of the community. So I don't think we can undo the past. In fact, the past is going to be with us for a good many years in uneducated men and women who lost their chance for a decent education. We have to do the best we can now. That is what we are trying to do. I don't think quotas are a good idea. I think it is a mistake to begin to assign quotas on the basis of religion or race or color, or nationality.

"I think we get into a good deal of trouble. Our whole view of ourselves is a sort of one society. That has not been true. At least that is where we are trying to go. I think that we ought not to begin the quota system. On the other hand, I do think that we ought to make an effort to give a fair chance to everyone who is qualified, not through a quota, but just look over our employment rolls, look over our areas where we are hiring people, and at least make sure we are giving everyone a fair chance, but not hard-and-fast quotas. We are too mixed, this society of ours, to begin to divide ourselves on the basis of race or color."

On tax cuts, in a 1962 speech Kennedy said: "It is a paradoxical truth that tax rates are too high today and tax revenues are too low, and the soundest way to raise the revenues in the long run is to cut the rates now. ... The purpose of cutting taxes now is not to incur a budget deficit but to achieve the more prosperous, expanding economy, which can bring a budget surplus."

On dealing with foreign enemies, JFK believed, as Reagan did, in peace through strength, not strength through peace. In his inaugural address, Kennedy said, "Let every nation know, whether it wishes us well or ill, that we shall pay any price, bear any burden, meet any hardship, support any friend, oppose any foe to assure the survival and the success of liberty."

On the Second Amendment, this lifetime member of the NRA believed it conferred an *individual right* to keep and bear arms. In 1961, Kennedy said: "Today we need a nation of minutemen: citizens who are not only prepared to take up arms, but citizens who regard the preservation of freedom as a basic purpose of their daily life and who are willing to consciously work and sacrifice for that freedom. The cause of liberty, the cause of America, cannot succeed with any lesser effort."

Abortion was not an issue during the 1960 presidential campaign. Nor was it an issue during his presidency. Kennedy did say this: "Now, on the question of limiting population: As you know, the Japanese have been doing it very vigorously, through abortion, which I think would be repugnant to all Americans."

In 1971, in a letter to a constituent, John Kennedy's brother, Sen. Ted Kennedy, wrote: "It is my personal feeling that the legalization of abortion on demand is not in accordance with the value which our civilization places on human life. Wanted or unwanted, I believe that human life, even at its earliest stages, has certain rights which must be recognized — the right to be born, the right to love, the right to grow old. ... Once life has begun, no matter at what stage of growth, it is my belief that termination should not be decided merely by desire."

On guns, taxes, racial preferences, foreign policy and abortion, John F. Kennedy would not be comfortable in today's Democratic Party. He was, after all, a Kennedy Democrat.

Trump Eviscerates the Liberal Media — What Took So Long?

February 23, 2017

It was riveting. In his first solo press conference, President Donald Trump spent much of the hour berating the media for what Trump called anti-Republican bias and its relentlessly negative "tone."

It's about time. The liberal media has long been sticking it to Republicans.

In October 1992, during the presidential race between President George H. W. Bush and Bill Clinton, Investor's Business Daily found that over 90 percent of the economic news in newspapers was negative. At the time, the economy was well into a recovery, on its 19th consecutive month of growth. Yet much of the business news was sour.

The next month, November 1992, Bill Clinton won. Investor's Business Daily found that suddenly only 14 percent of the newspapers' economic news was negative, a dramatic decline in negativity and upswing in positive economic news.

ABC News' Peter Jennings, NBC's Tom Brokaw and CBS' Dan Rather anchored the nightly news for the then-"Big Three" networks on the first day in office of both Presidents Bill Clinton and George W. Bush. On Clinton's first day in office, he reversed a President Ronald Reagan policy forbidding the use of federal money for abortions. President Bush reversed Bill Clinton's reversal.

So how did networks cover each president's first day on their evening news broadcasts?

Peter Jennings, ABC News, 1993: "President Clinton *kept a promise* (emphasis added) today on the 20th anniversary of the Supreme Court decision legalizing abortion. Mr. Clinton signed presidential memoranda rolling back many of the restrictions imposed by his predecessors."

Peter Jennings and Terry Moran, ABC News, 2001: "President Bush begins by taking a tough line on abortion," said Jennings in a teaser for the story. Moran then reported: "One of the president's first actions was designed to *appeal to anti-abortion conservatives* (emphasis added). The president signed an order reinstating a Reagan-era policy that prohibited federal funding of family planning groups that provided abortion counseling services overseas."

Tom Brokaw, "NBC Nightly News," 1993: "Today, President Clinton *kept a campaign promise* (emphasis added), and it came on the 20th anniversary of Roe v. Wade legalizing abortion."

Tom Brokaw, "NBC Nightly News," 2001: "We'll begin with the new president's very active day, which started on a *controversial note* (emphasis added)."

Dan Rather, CBS News, 1993: "Today, with the stroke of a pen, President Clinton *delivered on his campaign promise* (emphasis added) to cancel several anti-abortion regulations of the Reagan-Bush years."

Dan Rather, CBS News, 2001: "This was President Bush's first day at the office, and he did something to quickly *please the right flank* (emphasis added) in his party: He reinstituted an anti-abortion policy."

Here's another example.

The media routinely refers to the recession President Barack Obama inherited as the "great recession." But during the recession President Reagan dealt with, unemployment hit 10.8 percent, versus Obama's peak of 10.0 percent. During Reagan's presidency, prime interest rates hit 20.5 percent, and inflation, which was modest under Obama, averaged 13.5 percent under Reagan in the early '80s.

Reagan lowered taxes, continued deregulation and slowed down the rate of domestic spending. Obama, of course, did the opposite.

The left thinks that, as with Obama, President Franklin Delano Roosevelt's active intervention in the economy "rescued" it from the Great Depression. Many economists strongly disagree. William H.

Peterson of the Heritage Foundation says, "The Great Depression sprang from three fatal mistakes — the Fed's jacking up of money-supply growth in the 1920s, which fueled the stock market boom; the Smoot-Hawley Tariff of 1930, hiking import duties to their highest level in U.S. history and inviting deadly foreign retaliation against U.S. exports; and the Revenue Act of 1932, hiking the top income-tax rate from 24 percent to 63 percent."

In "Out of Work," a book about unemployment in 20th century America, economists Richard Vedder and Lowell Gallaway say, "The common interpretation is that this Depression, this misery, this inequality, reflected rigidities and imperfections in the markets for goods and resources. Yet the evidence we have presented is more consistent with a far different story. The market, particularly the critical market for labor, was prevented from operating in a normal fashion by the interventions of government. These intrusions turned a severe shock that started a recession into a major depression. Government failure, not market failure, was the problem."

Consider what Roosevelt's secretary of treasury, Henry Morgenthau Jr., wrote in his diary: "We have tried spending money. We are spending more than we have ever spent before and it does not work. ... I want to see this country prosperous. I want to see people get a job. I want to see people get enough to eat. We have never made good on our promises. ... I say after eight years of this Administration we have just as much unemployment as when we started and an enormous debt to boot!" Yet high school textbooks teach us that government spending, what the left today calls government "investments," pulled the economy for the abyss.

To reverse media bias, President Trump has his work cut out for him. But his press conference was a good start.

The Oscars: The Activism They Left on the Cutting Room Floor

March 2, 2017

Imagine the result, with hundreds of millions of people watching worldwide, if Hollywood turned its creative firepower on real problems. Instead, viewers watched wall-to-wall Trump-bashing. They should have spent less time bashing Trump and more time making the sure presenters got the correct envelopes. If so, the Oscar gaffe of the century — reading the wrong name for Best Picture — might have been avoided. Also, during the "In Memoriam" portion of the night, they put up picture of a very much alive producer instead of the costume designer who died last October. The broadcast's ratings were the second-lowest in Academy Award history. No doubt many anticipated the Trump smackdown, and decided to respond with a smackdown of their own. It's called not watching.

Not one word was said about the oppression and subjugation of women in parts of the Muslim and Arab world. Nothing was said about how women, in parts of the Arab and Muslim world, cannot work outside the home, drive a car or get a divorce. There are instances in which a Muslim woman, having been raped, becomes a criminal for having had sex with someone other than her husband. Not one word was said about radical Islam, and nothing about ISIS, Boko Haram, al-Qaida, Hamas, Hezbollah or other terror groups.

The winner of Best Foreign Film declined to travel from Iran to attend the Oscars because, as he put it in the statement read on stage: "I'm sorry I'm not with you tonight. My absence is out of respect for the people of my country and those of other six nations who have been disrespected by the inhumane law that bans entry of immigrants to the U.S. Dividing the world into the 'us' and 'our enemies' categories creates fear — a deceitful justification for aggression and war. These wars prevent democracy and human rights in countries which have themselves been victims of aggression. Filmmakers can turn their cameras to capture shared human qualities and break stereotypes of various nationalities and religions. They create empathy between us and others. An empathy which we need today more than ever."

Not one word about the fact that Iran leads the world as a state sponsor of terrorism. Nothing about how the ayatollahs and Iranian politicians routinely chant, "Death to America" and, of course, "Death to Israel." Nothing about the fact that homosexuality is a crime in many Muslim and Arab countries. And in many of these countries — including some in Africa and Asia — the penalty for same-sex sexual acts is death. When the then-president of Iran, Mahmoud Ahmadinejad, spoke at Columbia University in 2007, he was asked to explain the execution of homosexuals in Iran. Ahmadinejad denied homosexuals even existed in his country: "In Iran we don't have homosexuals like in your country. In Iran we do not have this phenomenon. I don't know who's told you that we have this."

Hollywood's silence over the abusive treatment of women, gays and religious minorities in much of the Muslim and Arab world has a parallel in academia. Dr. Fred Gottheil is an economics professor at the University of Illinois. In January 2009, Gottheil found a four-page petition, signed by 900 academics, calling for a U.S. abandonment of the support of Israel. Many petition signatories, he discovered after further research, were faculty in women's and gender studies departments. What about the anti-human rights, anti-gay, anti-woman practices in the Muslim Middle East?

Gottheil wrote a four-page "Statement of Concern" about human rights violations in the Muslim Middle East, such as honor killing, wife-beating, female genital mutilation and violence against gays and lesbians. His statement included evidence of such atrocities and included the names of Muslim clerics and scholars defending these human rights violations. He sent the statement to 675 signers of the anti-Israel petition, and asked for their support. "The results were surprising," Gottheil said, "even though I thought the responses would be few. They were almost nonexistent. ...What conclusions do I draw from this? The academic leftists are caught in an ideologically discriminatory trap of their own making. It turns out that with all their professing profession of principle, they are sanctimonious bigots at heart. And some are so obsessed about Israel that they would undermine their own self-interest. Witness the faculty in gender studies who signed the anti-Israel petition but didn't sign my 'Statement of Concern' which is about discrimination of women, gays, and lesbians in the Muslim Middle East. Sort of pathetic, actually."

On Oscar night, when the Hollywood community could have shed light on these atrocities, they were in busy bashing Trump — in la-la land.

Obamacare Can't Be 'Fixed'

March 9, 2017

The moment Republicans bought into the notion that Obamacare must not just be repealed but "replaced," Democrats won. Democrats argue that health care is a "right." Republicans claim they disagree, that nowhere in the Constitution does the federal government guarantee health care treatment or health care insurance. But Republicans' behavior suggests otherwise.

President Donald Trump, for example, says that in replacing Obamacare no one should be worse off; that insurance companies cannot decline those with pre-existing medical conditions; that insurance carriers must allow parents to keep their "children" on their insurance plans until the age of 26; and that insurance companies cannot drop people under any circumstances. Polls show that these are the most popular features of Obamacare. But forcing an insurance company to cover people with pre-existing conditions completely destroys the concept of insurance. Insurance is about pooling groups of people whose premiums cover unknown risks, not known ones.

The "replacement" plan runs head-on against two principles of economics. Competition makes products and services better, cheaper and more accessible. And there's no such thing as a free lunch.

Health care — just like cars, sweaters and smartphones — is a commodity. But health care is one of our most regulated industries, a far cry from a free-market-based system.

Start with the supply of doctors. Because of regulations, the supply of doctors has been artificially limited. Economist Milton

Friedman once compared the American Medical Association to a medieval guild that shuts out would-be practitioners and artificially protects the wages of doctors. In a piece called "American Medical Association: The Strongest Trade Union in the U.S.A.," Mark Perry, a professor of economics and finance at the University of Michigan and an American Enterprise Institute scholar, writes:

"Between about 1970 and 1984, there was a significant increase in medical school graduates that pushed the number of new physicians from 4 per 100,000 Americans in 1970 to almost 7 per 100,000 by 1984. Since 1984, the number of medical school graduates has been relatively flat ... while the population has continued to grow, causing the number of new physicians per 100,000 population to decline to only 5.3 per 100,000 by 2008, the same ratio as back in 1974. Over the last few years the number of medical school graduates has increased slightly, and the ratio of graduates per 100,000 increased to 5.56 last year, the highest in a decade."

What's wrong with this picture? An aging population, in need of *more* doctors, on a per capita basis, has *fewer* of them. Economics 101, supply and demand and plain common sense tell us the opposite should be happening.

This is the argument Republicans should be making. The true replacement plan should be loosening regulations that prevent would-be doctors from entering the field, and prevent less-schooled and less-credentialed paraprofessionals from doing things that only licensed doctors can now do.

We train battlefield medics in Iraq and Afghanistan to deal with battlefield trauma, saving countless lives. The Oscar-nominated film "Hacksaw Ridge" depicted the true story of a medic with aspirations of becoming a doctor, whom the army trained to treat battlefield injuries. But that man, had he returned stateside and tried to set up a practice to treat victims of urban gun violence, would have been guilty of practicing medicine without a license.

There are many examples. In some states midwives cannot legally deliver babies, despite ample evidence that they possess the experience and ability. In his joint address to Congress, Trump criticized the lengthy and expensive process of getting a drug approved by the FDA. In some cases, drugs that could help people do not become available even when risks are known and desperate patients would be willing to assume these risks.

We strangle the health care and insurance industries with regulations, licensure requirements and barriers to entry that artificially increase the cost of health care. We prevent people from buying health care across state lines.

We advise developing countries to follow the well-worn path to prosperity — free markets, free trade, rule of law and property rights. Yet when it comes to nearly one-seventh of our economy — health care — we ignore our own advice. For health care, we don't write ourselves the proper prescription.

When Obama Compared Slaves to Immigrants, He Got Applause; Carson Gets Called 'Uncle Tom'

March 16, 2017

Dr. Ben Carson, in a speech before employees of Housing and Urban Development, the department he now runs, likened slaves to "immigrants": "That's what America is about, a land of dreams and opportunity. There were other immigrants who came here in the bottom of slave ships, worked even longer, even harder, for less. But they, too, had a dream that one day their sons, daughters, grandsons, granddaughters, great-grandsons, great-granddaughters, might pursue prosperity and happiness in this land."

Carson got hammered.

Late-night comic Trevor Noah said: "It makes them sound like they work at Wal-Mart. ... Calling slaves 'immigrants' is like saying: 'It's not kidnapping. That person just got a free vacation in a basement.' ... Slaves weren't immigrants. Because an immigrant has choice. They choose the country they're going to because they hope it will bring them a better life. Saying that slaves are just another group of immigrants erases how black people were uniquely oppressed in America. It helps justify blaming African-Americans for their hardships."

Actor Samuel L. Jackson tweeted: "OK!! Ben Carson ... I can't! Immigrants? In the bottom of SLAVE SHIPS??!! MUTHAF——PLEASE!!! #d—-headedtom."

Actress Whoopi Goldberg said: "Were the slaves really thinking about the American dream? No, because they were thinking, 'What the hell just happened?!' You know, when people immigrate, they come with the idea that they're going someplace for a better life. ... It's voluntary. ... How does he miss what slavery is?! How does he miss that no slave came to this country willingly? ... Ben, 'Roots.' Watch 'Roots.'"

TV personality Star Jones tweeted: "No way in the world he is that friggin ignorant." Using the pile-of-excrement emoji, she called the renowned neurosurgeon "(expletive) for brains." She ended the tweet: "#UncleTom thy name is #BenCarson."

Rep. Keith Ellison, D-Minn., insists that Carson's "slave equals immigrant" perspective means he is unqualified to lead HUD because Carson "doesn't know how urgent it is to confront racism" in housing: "It's disturbing to me, and it should be to every American, not just black Americans. ... For him, the HUD secretary, to have a stunning misunderstanding of history like that, is really, really striking. ... And so for the HUD secretary not to get that means that he doesn't know how urgent it is to confront racism and discrimination in housing, which is a very scary thing for the HUD secretary to not understand."

Following the uproar, Carson posted this clarification on Facebook: "The slave narrative and immigrant narrative are two entirely different experiences. ... The two experiences should never be intertwined, nor forgotten, as we demand the necessary progress towards an America that's inclusive and provides access to equal opportunity for all."

One slight problem.

The "insensitive" and "demeaning" slave-equals-immigrant argument was made on a number of occasions by President Barack Obama: "It wasn't always easy for new immigrants," Obama said at a 2015 naturalization ceremony for new citizens. "Certainly it wasn't easy for those of African heritage who had not come here voluntarily, and yet in their own way were immigrants themselves. There was discrimination and hardship and poverty. But, like you, they no doubt found inspiration in all those who had come before them. And they were able to muster faith that, here in America, they might build a better life and give their children something more."

Even "Daily Show" host Noah admitted, "President Obama said something similar in 2015." But, said Noah, "You could tell before (Obama) said that part he was thinking, 'Damn, my speechwriter f—-ed up.'"

In fact, according to the Federalist, Obama likened slaves to immigrants on 11 different occasions. "Whether our ancestors landed on Ellis Island," said Obama, "or came here on a slave ship or crossed the Rio Grande, we are all connected to one another. We rise and fall together."

Goldberg, Noah, Jackson and Ellison were obviously occupied the 11 times Obama showed he "doesn't know how urgent it is to confront racism."

Why the silence over Obama's many slave-equals-immigrant comments versus the desk pounding by the same critics when Carson says the same thing? Carson represents an existential threat to the left. He is deadly to their cause — a black man, raised in poverty by a hardworking, welfare-abstaining single mom who taught her children to embrace hard work and education. The left believes that blacks are perpetual victims of slavery, Jim Crow and racism. It is vital for the existence of the Democratic Party to convince blacks to vote like victims in need of protection from the racist, sexist retrogrades known as Republicans. So black conservatives like Carson, who argues that welfare creates dependency, who demands choice in K-12 education and who believes hard work wins, must be attacked, marginalized and dismissed as "against their own people."

What to Do About Obamacare and the Uninsurable? Free Markets and Charity!

March 23, 2017

When it comes to repealing and replacing Obamacare, defenders of President Barack Obama's signature domestic law constantly ask, "What about those with pre-existing illnesses?"

After all, the most popular feature of Obamacare is that it prohibits insurance companies from denying coverage because an applicant has a pre-existing illness. And President Donald Trump and House Speaker Paul Ryan insist that those with pre-existing conditions will be covered. But by agreeing with Obama on the issue of pre-existing illnesses, by promising to replace Obamacare "with something better," Republicans are making a massive concession: That access to health care insurance should be guaranteed by the federal government, and that denying people coverage based on their health history is unfair and should be prevented by law.

That's a lot for the supposedly limited-government party to buy into. Free markets are the best way to improve quality, accessibility and affordability. But by campaigning to "repeal and replace" Obamacare, by refusing to make the case that free markets beat government-controlled health care, they've done just that. So the question now simply becomes who pays and how much.

When did health insurance become a right?

Did the Founding Fathers, under Article I, Section 8, grant the federal government the power and duty to ensure "universal health care coverage"? The answer is no, and there are many historical examples that prove it.

Economist Walter Williams writes of Presidents James Madison, Franklin Pierce and Grover Cleveland, and how they quoted the Constitution to turn away congressional attempts to spend money when the federal government is not authorized to do so.

James Madison, known as the "father of the Constitution," opposed a 1792 bill that would appropriate $15,000 for French refugees. Madison said, "I cannot undertake to lay my finger on that article of the Constitution which granted a right to Congress of expending, on objects of benevolence, the money of their constituents."

Some argued that the Constitution allows for benevolent spending under the general-welfare clause. Not so, said Madison: "With respect to the words 'general welfare,' I have always regarded them as qualified by the detail of powers (enumerated in the Constitution) connected with them. To take them in a literal and unlimited sense would be a metamorphosis of the Constitution into a character which there is a host of proofs was not contemplated by its creators."

Later presidents understood this. President Pierce, in 1854, vetoed a bill meant to help the mentally ill, saying, "I cannot find any authority in the Constitution for public charity." To approve such spending, he said, "would be contrary to the letter and the spirit of the Constitution and subversive to the whole theory upon which the Union of these States is founded."

In 1887, President Cleveland vetoed a bill to send money to drought-stricken counties in Texas, saying: "I feel obliged to withhold my approval of the plan to indulge in benevolent and charitable sentiment through the appropriation of public funds. ... I find no warrant for such an appropriation in the Constitution."

This brings us back to the issue of those with pre-existing illnesses. Before Obamacare, 35 states had "high-risk pools" so that their residents with pre-existing illnesses could get non-group health insurance. But what about states that don't have high-risk pools? And even in states that do, some people will not be able to afford it, even at a reduced and subsidized price. What to do?

The answer is charity.

Alexis de Tocqueville, the Frenchman who spent months studying America in the 19th century, wrote this about America's charitable spirit: "Americans group together to hold fetes, found seminaries, build inns, construct churches, distribute books, dispatch missionaries to the antipodes. They establish hospitals, prisons, schools by the same method. Finally, if they wish to highlight a truth or develop an opinion by the encouragement of a great example, they form an association."

As for why Americans donate so much to charity, Tocqueville considered it a matter of enlightened self-interest: "American moralists do not claim that one must sacrifice oneself for one's fellows because it is a fine thing to do but they are bold enough to say that such sacrifices are as necessary to the man who makes them as to those gaining from them. ... They do not, therefore, deny that every man can pursue his own self-interest but they turn themselves inside out to prove that it is in each man's interest to be virtuous. ... Enlightened self-love continually leads them to help one another and inclines them to devote freely a part of their time and wealth to the welfare of the state."

Life is not fair. But it is unfair to assume that an America without a government-provided safety net would turn its backs on the less fortunate. Charity is in America's DNA.

Obamacare Was Designed to Explode — Dems Want Single-Payer

March 30, 2017

There were two big winners when the House failed to take up the President Donald Trump-backed bill to repeal and replace Obamacare: Barack Obama, who saw Obamacare stand; and Dr. Ben Carson, who was smart enough to pick Housing and Urban Development over Health and Human Services.

Oh, spare us the "Republicans failed to get their health care bill through" media hyperventilation. Trump, said many in the media with unconcealed glee, did not close the deal! The Trump agenda is imperiled! Had it passed, the same pundits would be shredding it as cold and heartless, the moral equivalent of signing your granny up with ISIS just to get her out of the house.

Yes, despite a Republican in the Oval Office and Republican majorities in the Senate and House, Trump and Speaker Paul Ryan couldn't pressure that faction of "free-market Republicans" known as the Freedom Caucus to sign on to their Obamacare replacement. This must be frustrating to the businessman-turned-politician in chief.

Historian Richard E. Neustadt, in "Presidential Power: the Politics of Leadership" writes: "When contemplating General Eisenhower winning the Presidential election, Truman said, 'He'll sit here, and he'll say, 'Do this! Do that!' And nothing will happen. Poor Ike — it won't be a bit like the Army. He'll find it very frustrating.'" No doubt, Trump is experiencing this frustration.

Reportedly, Trump recently lamented that real estate is easier than politics.

As for Obamacare, Trump is right to point out that Obamacare is on life support right now, and rising premiums, copays and deductibles were forecast even if Hillary Clinton had won the presidency. Remember, too, that Obamacare was intended to "fail," given the Democrats' real goal of a Canadian-style taxpayer-paid health care. Harry Reid openly said so. The Las Vegas Sun reported in 2013:

"In just about seven weeks, people will be able to start buying Obamacare-approved insurance plans through the new health care exchanges.

"But already, Senate Majority Leader Harry Reid is predicting those plans, and the whole system of distributing them, will eventually be moot.

"Reid said he thinks the country has to 'work our way past' insurance-based health care during a Friday night appearance on Vegas PBS' program 'Nevada Week in Review.'

"'What we've done with Obamacare is have a step in the right direction, but we're far from having something that's going to work forever,' Reid said.

"When then asked by panelist Steve Sebelius whether he meant ultimately the country would have to have a health care system that abandoned insurance as the means of accessing it, Reid said: 'Yes, yes. Absolutely, yes.'"

Former Democratic National Committee Chair Howard Dean also said the end game is the so-called "public option." During the 2008 presidential campaign, Dean talked about the health care proposals of Democratic candidates Barack Obama and Sen. Hillary Clinton: "I think while someday we may end up with a single-payer system, it's clear that we're not going to do it all at once, so I think both candidates' health care plans are a big step forward."

Obama, then a state senator from Illinois, said: "I happen to be a proponent of a single-payer, universal health care program. I see no reason why the United States of America, the wealthiest country in the history of the world, spending 14 percent of its gross national product on health care, cannot provide basic health insurance to everybody. ... A single-payer health care plan, a universal health care plan. That's what I'd like to see. But as all of you know, we may not get there immediately. Because first we've got to take back the White House, we've got to take back the Senate, and we've got to take back the House." And later then-presidential candidate Obama reiterated his stance, that if "starting from scratch" he'd have a single-payer system.

One more thing about Trump's new neighborhood, Washington, D.C. Trump talks about "draining the swamp" of the special-interest groups that have the city crawling with lobbyists. But the First Amendment recognizes the "right to redress grievances." This means lobbying. Big government means a big swamp that attracts those who seek to influence legislation and regulation to their benefit. Indeed, businesses have a fiduciary obligation to ensure that a given measure benefits them or that its potential harm be minimized. If we don't want lobbyists buzzing around, give them nothing to lobby about.

Welcome, Mr. President. You're not in New York anymore.

Trump Derangement Syndrome

April 6, 2017

President Donald Trump's daughter Ivanka, at the Republican National Convention in Cleveland, said she wanted to require companies to provide paid maternity leave. The President later reaffirmed that pledge, promising six weeks of paid leave for new mothers. His "fair trade" position is practically indistinguishable from that of Bernie Sanders. He wants taxpayers to "invest" in a trillion-dollar infrastructure program, something that even the Democratic leader of the Senate, Chuck Schumer, said he could get behind.

Trump wants to preserve the "good parts" of Obamacare, including preventing insurance companies from denying coverage for pre-existing conditions. He said that government could use its eminent-domain power to seize private property for *private* development projects. On many occasions, Trump said he wants to "save" Medicare and Social Security. When asked to name the "top three functions" of the federal government, then-candidate Trump said "security for our nation," "health care" and "education." At the federal level? Not exactly Reaganesque, is it?

The man, on many issues, is a populist.

Yet the left's contempt for Trump was on full display in a recent speech by newly elected Democratic National Committee Chairman Tom Perez. Praising protestors who marched on the day after Trump's inauguration — calling it the day "the resistance took over" — Perez said: "They marched all over the world and said, 'Donald Trump, you don't stand for our values! ... Donald Trump, you didn't win this election!'" He called Trump a "bully," and belittled the President for "wanting his name on everything." Perez thundered: "(Republicans) don't give a s—- about people!"

Rep. Maxine Waters, the longtime California lefty, has all but impeached Trump. About Trump's friends, advisers and members of his administration: "I just think the American people had better understand what's going on. This is a bunch of scumbags — that's what they are — who are all organized around making money."

On the House floor, Waters slammed Trump supporters as less patriotic than blacks: "African-Americans have struggled and fought historically. Many African-Americans have paid a huge price fighting for justice and equality in this country, have died for it. ... When we fight against this President, and we point out how dangerous he is for this society and for this country, we're fighting for the democracy. We're fighting for America. We're saying to those who say they're patriotic, but they've turned a blind eye to the destruction that he's about to cause this country, 'You're not nearly as patriotic as we are.'"

When a former British spy wrote a dossier on Donald Trump — later published on Buzzfeed — that included some unproven accusations about Trump and a group of hookers, the hysterical Waters said: "We already know that the part about the coverage that they have on him, with sex actions, is supposed to be true. They have said that that's absolutely true. ... I think they should go into that dossier and see what's there." Waters never clarified who "they" are, or explained how she knew it to be true when mainstream media never touched the dossier story, Buzzfeed said it was "unverified" and even NBC's Chuck Todd accused Buzzfeed of publishing a "fake news" story.

Then there is comedian Chelsea Handler, who said: "I think the way we have come together is so inspiring. I would have hoped that would have happened before the election, but I'll f—-ing take it because it's so much better to be friends with people you would never talk to before just because we all know that Donald Trump is a f—-ing loser."

Comedian Tina Fey took the tactic of shaming white women who voted for Trump: "The thing that I keep focusing on is the idea that we sort of need to hold the edges, that it's sort of like a lot of this election was turned by ... white college-educated women who would now maybe like to forget about this election and go back to watching HGTV. ... I would want to urge them to — like, 'You can't look away, because it doesn't affect you this minute, but it's going to affect you eventually.'"

But Trump got a *lower* percentage of the white vote than did Mitt Romney. So why didn't Fey attack the black voters who voted for Trump in a greater percentage than for any Republican since Gerald Ford? Because that would have required the Hollywood liberal to go after blacks, some of whom voted twice for Obama. That's a tough putt.

Handler and Fey are comedians. But when it comes to Trump Derangement Syndrome, it's hard to tell the comics from the politicians.

Obama Claimed 'All' of Syria's Chemical Weapons Had Been Eliminated

April 13, 2017

The Obama administration claimed that it negotiated with Syria and Russia to eliminate "100 percent" of Syria's chemical weapons. After President Barack Obama's 2012 "red line" warning to Syria about using chemical weapons, Syria launched a chemical attack in August 2013. But U.S. military action was avoided by the alleged Russian/American/Syrian diplomatic accomplishment, achieved without "firing a shot." Here's what we were told:

President Obama, on April 28, 2014: "We're getting chemical weapons out of Syria without having initiated a strike."

Sen. Claire McCaskill, D-Mo., crowed on June 1, 2014: "We're getting the chemical weapons out of Syria." And Sen. Bob Casey, D-Pa., chimed in July 6: "We should commend the administration for the result that they got."

Then-Secretary of State John Kerry, on July 20, 2014: "We got 100 percent of the chemical weapons out (of Syria)."

President Obama, on Aug. 18, 2014: "Today we mark an important achievement in our ongoing effort to counter the spread of weapons of mass destruction by eliminating Syria's declared chemical weapons stockpile."

Kerry on Oct. 31, 2014: "We ... cut the deal that got 100 percent of the declared chemical weapons out of Syria, and people nevertheless have been critical — of one day of bombing versus the virtue of getting 100 percent of the chemical weapons out of Syria."

Kerry reiterated the accomplishment on Feb. 24, 2015, telling the Senate Foreign Relations Committee: "We got, as you know, last year, all the chemical weapons out of Syria."

True, Bloomberg reported on May 13, 2015: "The U.S. government was informed months ago that an international monitoring body found traces of chemical weapons that President Bashar al-Assad had promised to turn over, including sarin gas — a clear violation of the deal he struck with President Obama after crossing the administration's 'red line' two years ago.

"Officials from the Organization for the Prohibition of Chemical Weapons told the Obama administration early this year that its inspectors had found traces of two banned chemical weapons during an inspection of the Syrian government's Scientific Studies and Research Center in the district of Barzeh near Damascus, two administration officials told us. A report by Reuters May 8 said that OPCW inspectors had found traces of sarin and VX nerve agent at the site in separate inspections in December and January."

After the Bloomberg story, then-White House press secretary John Earnest initially admitted: "We're aware that the OPCW continues to receive credible allegations that the use of chemical weapons in Syria is still taking place." But a month later, on June 17, 2015, Earnest responded: "(Syria's) declared chemical weapons stockpile that Assad previously denied existed has now been acknowledged, rounded up, removed from the country and destroyed precisely because of the work of this administration and our successful efforts to work with the Russians to accomplish that goal."

But Susan Rice, then Obama's national security adviser, on Jan. 16, 2017, said, "We were able to find a solution that didn't necessitate the use of force that actually removed the chemical weapons that were known from Syria, in a way that the use of force would never have accomplished. ... We were able to get the Syrian government to voluntarily and verifiably give up its chemical weapons stockpile."

After last week's chemical weapons attack that left nearly 100 Syrians dead, former Obama advisers now say they always knew that not all of chemical weapons were eliminated — and that turning over all their weapons is not exactly what tyrants tend to do.

Antony J. Blinken, a former deputy secretary of state, recently said, "We always knew we had not gotten everything, that the Syrians had not been fully forthcoming in their declaration."

Michael McFaul, Obama's former ambassador to Russia, said, "For me, this tragedy underscores the dangers of trying to do deals with dictators without a comprehensive, invasive and permanent inspection regime."

Tom Malinowski, an assistant secretary of state for human rights under Obama, laments: "The difficult and debatable choice the Obama administration ... made not to use military force when Assad last used nerve gas against his people (in 2013) will shape our thinking about this and similar crises for a long time to come. The lesson I would draw from that experience is that when dealing with mass killing by unconventional or conventional means, deterrence is more effective than disarmament."

This brings us the Obama's Iran deal that allegedly prevents Iran from acquiring a nuclear weapon. Why should we believe that Obama was any less duped here than when he claimed the elimination of "all" of Syria's chemical weapons?

We shouldn't.

The Shameless Sean Spicer
Hitler Hypocrisy

April 20, 2017

Press secretary Sean Spicer publicly apologized several times for this comment about Bashar Assad, the murderous dictator of Syria: "You had someone as despicable as Hitler who didn't even sink to using chemical weapons." Spicer got hammered for supposedly minimizing the horror of the Holocaust.

MSNBC's Chris Matthews, in 2013, made the exact same comment about Syria's Assad: "It's been enforced in the Western community, around the world — international community for decades — don't use chemical weapons. We didn't use them in World War II. Hitler didn't use them. We don't use chemical weapons. That's no deal." What, no outrage?

Democrats and liberal media routinely compare Republicans to Hitler and Nazis, and Republican policies to fascism. They've done so for decades. Here are just a few examples:

During the 1964 presidential race, Republican presidential candidate Barry Goldwater accepted an invitation to visit an American military installation located in Bavaria, Germany. On "CBS Evening News," hosted by Walter Cronkite, correspondent Daniel Schorr said: "It is now clear that Sen. Goldwater's interview with Der Spiegel, with its hard line appealing to right-wing elements in Germany, was only the start of a move to link up with his opposite numbers in Germany." When Goldwater accepted the Republican nomination, Democratic California Gov. Pat Brown said, "The stench of fascism is in the air."

After Republicans took control of the House in the mid-'90s, Rep. John Dingell, D-Mich., compared the newly conservative-controlled House to "the Duma and the Reichstag," referring to the legislature set up by Czar Nicholas II of Russia and the parliament of the German Weimar Republic that brought Hitler to power.

About President George W. Bush, billionaire Democratic contributor George Soros said, "(He displays the) supremacist ideology of Nazi Germany," and that his administration used rhetoric that echoes his childhood in occupied Hungary. "When I hear Bush say, 'You're either with us or against us,'" Soros said, "it reminds me of the Germans." He also said: "The (George W.) Bush administration and the Nazi and communist regimes all engaged in the politics of fear. ... Indeed, the Bush administration has been able to improve on the techniques used by the Nazi and Communist propaganda machines."

Former Vice President Al Gore claimed the Bush administration employed "digital" storm troopers, the paramilitary arm of Hitler's Nazi Party: "(George W. Bush's) executive branch has made it a practice to try and control and intimidate news organizations, from PBS to CBS to Newsweek. ... And every day, they unleash squadrons of digital brownshirts to harass and hector any journalist who is critical of the President."

NAACP Chairman Julian Bond played the Nazi card several times. Speaking at historically black Fayetteville State University in North Carolina in 2006, Bond said, "The Republican Party would have the American flag and the swastika flying side by side."

After the 2012 Republican National Convention, California Democratic Party Chairman John Burton said: "(Republicans) lie, and they don't care if people think they lie. As long as you lie, (Nazi propaganda minister) Joseph Goebbels — the big lie — you keep repeating it."

In 2012, then-Chairman of the South Carolina Democratic Party Dick Harpootlian compared the state's Republican governor to Hitler's mistress. When told that the Republicans were holding a competing press conference at a NASCAR Hall of Fame basement studio, Harpootlian told the South Carolina delegation, "(Gov. Nikki Haley) was down in the bunker, a la Eva Braun."

Following Donald Trump's election, Washington Post columnist David Ignatius invoked a comparison to the three-night murder spree in 1934 Germany carried out by the Nazi regime, saying about Trump's then-evolving transition team: "I think there is kind of a 'Night of the Long Knives' quality as this Trump team sorts out who is going to be on top, who is going to have the president-elect's ear."

Former Democratic National Committee Chairman Howard Dean said of then-President-elect Trump, "His ... senior adviser (Steve Bannon) is a Nazi. ... It's a big word. I don't usually use it unless somebody's really anti-Semitic, really misogynist, really anti-black."

Rep. Keith Ellison, D-Minn., the newly elected second-in-command at the Democratic National Committee, compared then-President George W. Bush and 9/11 to Adolf Hitler and the destruction of the Reichstag, the German parliament building: "9/11 is the juggernaut in American history and it allows ... it's almost like, you know, the Reichstag fire," Ellison said. "After the Reichstag was burned, they blamed the Communists for it, and it put the leader of that country (Hitler) in a position where he could basically have authority to do whatever he wanted."

The Spicer/Hitler-reference hysteria serves as just the latest example of left-wing hypocrisy, double standards and selective outrage.

Trump's Biggest Achievement in His 1st 100 Days? Stopping the Left

April 27, 2017

President Donald Trump's biggest achievement in his first 100 days? Easy. He stopped the left.

Measure Trump's first 100 days not just by looking at what he has or has not accomplished. Look at what America would have experienced under the alternative: Hillary Clinton.

Under Clinton, the debate would not be on how to replace Obamacare, but how quickly can the left realize its ultimate ambition, a Canadian-style, single-payer system. Under Clinton, the issue would not be how steep the tax cuts, but how many "rich" people, also known as job creators, would experience yet another growth-restricting tax hike.

Under Clinton, the $100 billion-plus annually in new regulations imposed by President Barack Obama — much of it to fight "climate change" — would continue to rise. This has stopped. President Trump signed an executive order that requires an elimination of two regulations for every new regulation proposed by an executive department or agency in 2017, with a zero-dollar net increase in the cost of regulations.

Under Clinton, newly confirmed conservative Justice Neil Gorsuch would've been another Ruth Bader Ginsburg/Sonia Sotomayor/Elena Kagan clone. Four left-wing SCOTUS justices, in the Heller case, ruled that there is not an individual right to keep and bear arms. Spare us a fifth one.

Trump, too, has put the left-wing media on notice. No more Mr. Nice Guy. Through WikiLeaks, we found that John Harwood, a debate moderator, emailed a letter to Hillary Clinton campaign manager John Podesta, bragging about a question he had put to Donald Trump. He also emailed advice on dealing with the challenge posed by Dr. Ben Carson. Staffers for newsmen Jake Tapper and Wolf Blitzer of CNN contacted the Democratic National Committee to seek questions they might put to Republican presidential candidates. There were many other examples of flat-out collusion, well beyond the liberal bias we've come to expect.

President Trump also changed eight years of Obama's "leading from behind" foreign policy by using our largest non-nuclear bomb on ISIS in Afghanistan and bombing Syria for its use of chemical weapons. Under Obama, we pulled out all the troops from Iraq, despite the objections of his foreign policy and national security and defense teams. One of the members of the Joint Chiefs of Staff, now-retired Army Gen. Ray Odierno, said: "I go back to the work we did in 2007 (through) 2010, and we got into a place that was really good. Violence was low, the economy was growing, politics looked like it was heading in the right direction. ... We thought we had it going exactly in the right direction, but now we watch it fall apart. It's frustrating. ... I think, maybe, if we had stayed a little more engaged, I think maybe it might have prevented it."

Under Obama, we bombed Libya, a mission that the Obama administration admitted was done for humanitarian reasons. Libyan dictator Moammar Gadhafi had paid reparations for the terrorist explosion of Pan Am Flight 103 over Lockerbie, Scotland. And following the American-led invasion of Iraq, Gadhafi had surrendered his weapons of mass destruction to the U.S. Yet under President Obama, America joined the French and British in bombing Libya to rid the country of Gadhafi. Incredibly, after criticizing President George W. Bush for not thinking through the invasion of Iraq, when Obama was asked what he thought was the "biggest mistake" of his presidency, Obama said, "Probably failing to plan for the day after what I think was the right thing to do in intervening in Libya."

For the most part, President Trump has delivered on his promises, or has attempted to deliver on them.

Take immigration. While the wall construction has not begun, nor has Trump been able to figure out a way to get Mexico to pay for it, a psychological wall has already gone up. Border-crossing apprehensions were down more than 60 percent from January to March, after Trump made it clear the welcome mat for illegal entry has been rolled up.

As for the so-called "failure" to repeal and replace Obamacare, businesspeople nevertheless have confidence that whatever emerges will be less expensive, less onerous and less intrusive than what they would have faced under a President Hillary Clinton.

Ultimately, Trump will likely be judged on one thing — the economy. If he manages a 4 percent GDP growth, as promised during the campaign, few will care about his nocturnal tweets.

After 100 days of Trump, the earth did not open up and swallow America. His critics can crawl out from under the bed. The stock market has hit record highs; small-business and consumer confidence polls show optimism in levels not seen anywhere from 10 to nearly 40 years, depending upon the poll. Something is happening.

When Ronald Reagan died, George Will wrote: "Today Americans gratefully recall that at a turbulent moment in their national epic, Reagan became the great reassurer, the steadying captain of our clipper ship. He calmed the passengers — and the sea."

It's not too soon to wonder whether someday something similar might be said of President Trump.

Parents: Prepare Your College Kids for Left-Wing Campus Bias

May 4, 2017

Do college students — and their parents — truly understand how thoroughly left-wing professors dominate the humanities side of academia?

Many people know that most professors are liberal, but the degree to which the left wing rules is jaw-dropping. A study published last September in Econ Journal Watch, "Faculty Voter Registration in Economics, History, Journalism, Law, and Psychology," documents the overwhelming left-wing nature of the voter registration of college profs at 40 leading universities. An examination of voter registration in five departments found that Democrats outnumber Republicans by 11 1/2-to-1. Even in economics, where one would think that views would be driven by data, not politics, Democrats outnumbered Republicans 4 1/2-to-1. History was practically foreign terrain for Republicans, as Democrats outnumbered them 33 1/2-to-1.

And it's getting worse. A 1968 study put the Democrat-to-Republican ratio in history departments at 2.7-to-1. This latest study found that among profs 65 and older, Democrats outnumber Republicans by 10 to 1. But for scholars under the age of 36 the ratio is 22.7-to-1.

In 2012 the California Association of Scholars published the results of a two-year study about the bias of professors in the University of California system. The study claims that professors' bias "corrupts" education, turning schools into indoctrination camps.

According to the National Association of Scholars: "The report documented curricula that promote political activism, in violation of UC regulations. For example, one course aims to be a 'training ground' for 'advocates committed to racial justice theory and practice.'" The CAS report also cited earlier studies that found that associate and assistant professors, those waiting in the wings, are ever more likely to be registered as Democrats. Among UC Berkeley's associates and assistants, said the report, registered Democrats outnumber registered Republicans by 49-to-1 in *all* departments — including sciences.

What about commencement speakers?

Of the political speakers, left-wingers dramatically outnumber conservatives. The student political advocacy group Campus Reform looked at last year's commencement speakers for the top 100 colleges and universities from U.S. News & World Report's annual ranking of best colleges. Of the then-announced speakers associated with political messages, 40 were liberal and 10 conservative, a ratio of 4-to-1 in favor of Democrats.

What about political contributions?

In the 2012 presidential election, a Campus Reform study found that 96 percent of the Ivy League's faculty and staffers who made campaign donations sent their checks to Barack Obama. At Brown University, just one professor contributed to Mitt Romney's campaign. Employees of the eight prestigious schools sent more than $1.2 million to President Obama, but contributed just $114,166 to Romney's campaign — a ratio of more than 10-to-1 in favor of Obama.

This brings us to what can only be described as Trump Derangement Syndrome, campus style. UC Berkeley claims, in effect, that it cannot protect students and property, therefore "incendiary" conservative speakers like Ann Coulter and David Horowitz — who actually attended graduate school there — had to cancel their proposed speeches. Meanwhile, at Claremont McKenna College in California, students blocked entry to those who came to hear pro-cop researcher Heather Mac Donald. "Activists" called Mac Donald a "white supremacist fascist," among other things, for researching and concluding that, no, cops are not engaging in illegal racial profiling. At Middlebury College, a professor who cosponsored the invitation to conservative Charles Murray, which prompted a riot, apologized — to the rioters! Another California human psychology professor called Trump's election "an act of terrorism."

Dartmouth recently conducted a field survey of nearly 500 of its students and found that 45 percent of the students who self-identified as Democrats said they would be "uncomfortable" rooming with a conservative, while only 12 percent of Republican students said that they would be "uncomfortable" with a liberal roommate.

The question is whether left-wing professors create left-wing students. To say there is no effect is to say teachers don't matter. Consider this. In an attempt to quantify the effect of media bias, UCLA economics and political science professor Tim Groseclose writes: "(The) average voter received approximately 8.2 percent of his news from Fox, and 79.9 percent from establishment media (defined as all outlets except Fox, the internet and talk radio). Thus, the 'reach' of establishment media is approximately 10 times that of Fox News." He says in presidential elections, liberal media bias gives Dems an advantage of eight to 10 points. Were the media truly fair and balanced, concludes Groseclose, the average state would vote the way Texas does.

Is it not reasonable to assume that professors have at least some measure of influence on their students? Have many professors crossed the line from education to indoctrination? Will opposing views be tolerated and respected? Does a student run a risk of facing grade retaliation by a Trump-hating poli-sci professor?

Campus activists have long complained about "microaggressions," for which they demand "safe spaces." Is there any place where a left-wing student can feel safer than a college campus, where conservatives are not just unwanted but cannot even speak?

Dear Jane Fonda: Minimum Wages Destroy Jobs

May 11, 2017

Dear Ms. Fonda:

Before you travel to Detroit this weekend to campaign for a $12 minimum wage, I suggest you read this letter.

I'm sure you mean well. But are you familiar with the voluminous number of peer-reviewed studies that conclude minimum-wage laws damaged the very people that many of the Hollywood left say they care about — blacks?

Respected economist David Neumark examined *all* of the major academic minimum-wage studies from the previous 20 years, more than 100 studies in all. Eighty-five percent of the studies found that minimum-wage laws destroy jobs, causing workers to lose jobs and/or hours or causing businesses to shut down. "Minimum-wage laws," said Neumark, have "a negative employment effect on low-skilled workers."

Believe it or not, before minimum-wage laws took effect, a black teenager was actually *more likely* to have a job than a white teen. I repeat — before the impact of federal minimum-wage laws, the first of which was in 1938, a black teen was more likely to be employed than a white teen. What happened?

Nobel-winning economist Milton Friedman calls the minimum-wage law "one of the most, if not the most, anti-black laws on the statute books." Friedman said: "The do-gooders believe that by passing a law saying that nobody shall get less than $2 an hour or $2.50 an hour, or whatever the minimum wage is, you are helping poor people who need the money. You are doing nothing of the kind. What you are doing is to assure that people whose skills are not sufficient to justify that kind of a wage will be unemployed. ...

"The minimum wage law is most properly described as a law saying employers must discriminate against people who have low skills. That's what the law says. The law says here's a man who ... has a skill which would justify a wage rate of $1.50, $2.00 an hour. You can't, you may not employ him. It's illegal. Because if you employ him you have to pay him $2.50. Well, what's the result? To employ him at $2.50 is to engage in charity. Now there's nothing wrong with charity. But most employers are not in a position where they can engage in that kind of charity. Thus the consequences of minimum-wage rates have been almost wholly bad, to increase unemployment and to increase poverty. Moreover, the effects have been concentrated on the groups that the do-gooders would most like to help. The people who have been hurt most by minimum-wage laws are the blacks."

Contrary to popular belief, most people on minimum wages are not men with families, but teenagers and part-time workers, and a disproportionately high percentage of them are young black and brown workers.

The Black Entertainment Television website, in 2011, published an article titled "Black Teens are Fired When the Minimum Wage Rises": "Economists William Even from Miami University and David Macpherson from Trinity University report that when a state, or the federal government, increases the minimum wage, black teens are more likely to be laid off. ... The report focused on 16- to 24-year-old males without a high school diploma and found that for each 10 percent increase in the federal or state minimum wage employment for young black males decreased 6.5 percent. By contrast, after the same wage boost, employment for white and Hispanic males fell respectively just 2.5 percent and 1.2 percent.

"The real hit for black teens occurred, however, in the 21 states that had the federal minimum wage increase in 2007, 2008 and 2009. The findings reveal that while 13,200 black young adults lost their jobs as a direct result of the recession nearly 40 percent more, a total of 18,500, were fired because of the rise in the federal minimum wage."

A new study on the minimum wage just came in. "Survival of the Fittest: The Impact of the Minimum Wage on Firm Exit" is by two researchers, one with Mathematica Policy Research and the other with Harvard Business School. It focused on whether a minimum wage increase also increased the likelihood of a restaurant shutting down as a result of the increased cost of labor. The researchers concluded that "a $1 increase in the minimum wage leads to approximately a 4 to 10 percent increase in the likelihood of exit." Not good.

Finally, even California Gov. Jerry Brown, who signed a $15 minimum-wage bill last year, conceded, "Economically, minimum wages may not make sense. But morally, and socially and politically, they make every sense because it binds the community together." Astonishing. Tell that to somebody who lost a job or failed to get one because of the minimum wage.

Have fun in Detroit, Ms. Fonda. Maybe instead of a speech, take in a Tigers game. You'll do a lot less damage.

Sincerely,

Larry Elder

Trump vs. Waters — Who Should Be Impeached?

May 18, 2017

Almost from the moment President Donald Trump recited the oath of office, Rep. Maxine Waters, D-Calif., began a quest for Trump's impeachment. But given Waters' record of 26 years in Congress (plus a prior 14 years in the California State Assembly), she should worry far more about the possibility of her own impeachment for leadership malpractice.

Here is a summary of some of her greatest hits:

Waters condemned the CIA for its alleged role in the creation of the Los Angeles-area drug problem, even though practically every major newspaper — The New York Times, the Los Angeles Times and The Washington Post — examined and rejected the charge. During a town hall meeting, she bellowed: "If I never do anything else in this career as a member of Congress, I'm gonna make somebody pay for what they've done to my community and to my people!"

The congresswoman's concern for the drug epidemic affecting "(her) people" apparently begins and ends in front of a microphone. In the '90s, a joint federal and local Houston DEA task force pursued cocaine-dealing allegations of James Prince, a childhood friend of Maxine Waters' husband. Waters wrote to then-Attorney General Janet Reno, calling the investigation racially motivated and demanding an end to the probe. She succeeded. One infuriated local DEA agent later publicly stated: "The Justice Department in Washington turned their backs on a good agent and a good investigation. It appears the object was to get them to stop their investigation, and it appears that worked."

In 1973, former Black Panther Joanne Chesimard shot and killed a New Jersey state trooper. Found guilty of murder and sentenced to life in prison, Chesimard escaped prison and fled to Cuba. Congress passed a resolution asking Fidel Castro to extradite her, but Waters wrote Castro a letter, urging him to let the "persecuted ... political activist" stay in Cuba and likening the cop killer to Martin Luther King, since Chesimard had been "persecuted for her civil rights work"!

Waters justified the 1992 Los Angeles riots by calling them a "rebellion," while bellowing, "No justice, no peace." The violence, she said, was "a spontaneous reaction to a lot of injustice and a lot of alienation and frustration." She defended looters: "There were mothers who took this as an opportunity to take some milk, to take some bread, to take some shoes. Maybe they shouldn't have done it, but the atmosphere was such that they did it. They are not crooks." Waters said: "One lady said her children didn't have any shoes. She just saw those shoes there, a chance for all of her children to have new shoes. Goddamn it! It was such a tear-jerker. I might have gone in and taken them for her myself."

Waters called President George H.W. Bush a "racist" and refused to apologize for it. She said of the then-sitting president: "I would like to ... say ... very clearly that I believe George (H.W.) Bush is a racist." She routinely refers to the Republican Party as "the enemy." She also referred to Republican former Los Angeles Mayor Richard Riordan as a "plantation owner." And she once proclaimed: "As far as I'm concerned, the tea party can go straight to hell."

Waters phoned then-Secretary of the Treasury Henry Paulson in 2008, asking his office to meet with financially distressed minority-owned banks. He complied. But most of the bankers in attendance were from OneUnited Bank — a bank in which Waters' husband owned shares and on whose board he once served. OneUnited asked for a special bailout, and a few months later it received $12 million. This prompted an investigation by the House ethics committee. The basis of the ethics inquiry was why Waters failed to disclose her personal financial interest in the bank bailout. After three years, the committee found no ethics violation, believing Waters' testimony that she did not know OneUnited was the distressed bank until after the meeting had taken place.

If Waters were a Republican, especially a white male Republican, the media would have long dismissed her as a racist, toxic, divisive demagogue. That the left — because of Waters' attacks on Trump — takes her seriously says far more about the left than about the President.

Great Moments in Fake News 'Journalism'

May 25, 2017

What about President Donald Trump's complaint about "fake news"? Let's look at some examples of "Great Moments in 'Journalism'" over the last few years.

Rep. Keith Ellison, D-Minn., in an appearance on ABC's Sunday morning political show hosted by George Stephanopoulos, called former Democratic Alabama Gov. George Wallace a "Republican." Ellison said, "At the same time, (in Trump) we do have the worst Republican nominee since George Wallace." Stephanopoulos either ignored or was ignorant of the fact that Wallace — who proudly proclaimed, "Segregation now, segregation tomorrow, segregation forever" — was a long-standing Democrat who served four terms as governor and twice sought the Democratic nomination for president. Tellingly, Stephanopoulos did not correct Ellison. Fortunately, another guest, Rep. Tom Cole, R-Okla., did correct the history-challenged Ellison.

Candy Crowley of CNN, one of the 2012 presidential debate moderators, "corrected" Mitt Romney when the Republican candidate accused President Barack Obama of failing to call the assault on Benghazi a "terror attack." Obama claimed he immediately called the assault on Benghazi an "act of terror":

Romney: "You said in the Rose Garden the day after the attack, it was an act of terror. It was not a spontaneous demonstration, is that what you're saying?"

Obama: "Please proceed, governor."

Romney: "I want to make sure we get that for the record because it took the president 14 days before he called the attack in Benghazi an act of terror."

Obama: "Get the transcript."

Crowley: "It — it — it — he did in fact, sir. So let me — let me call it an act of terror."

Obama: "Can you say that a little louder, Candy?"

Crowley: "He — he did call it an act of terror."

In truth, the day after the attack, Obama said: "No acts of terror will ever shake the resolve of this great nation, alter that character or eclipse the light of the values that we stand for." He only referred specifically to the deaths of four Americans in Libya as "an attack" or "this attack."

Fourteen days after the attack, Obama was asked: "I heard Hillary Clinton say it was an act of terrorism. Is it? What do you say?" The President responded: "We're still doing an investigation. There's no doubt that (with) the kind of weapons that were used, the ongoing assault, that it wasn't just a mob action. We don't have all the information yet, so we're still gathering it. But what's clear is that around the world, there's still a lot of threats out there." Clearly, Crowley was wrong when she "corrected" Romney and defended Obama. This was a turning point in the election.

MSNBC's Luke Russert, covering the 2008 presidential election, said students at the University of Virginia will vote Obama because: "You have to remember, the smartest kids in the state go there, so it's leaning a little bit towards Obama." Get it? Smart people vote Democrat. Dumb people vote Republican. Russert later apologized.

CNN's Carol Costello laughed hysterically as a frantic Bristol Palin, daughter of Sarah Palin, told cops she was assaulted at a party. Listen to how a gleeful Costello introduced the audiotape of Bristol describing the attack to the police: "This is quite possibly the best minute and a half of audio we've ever come across — well, come across in a long time, anyway. A massive brawl in Anchorage, Alaska, reportedly involving Sarah Palin's kids and her husband. It was sparked after someone pushed one of her daughters at a party. That's what Bristol Palin told police in an interview after the incident. ... So sit back and enjoy." A near-hysterical Palin says: "A guy comes out of nowhere and pushes me on the ground, takes me by my feet, in my dress — in my thong, dress, in front of everybody — 'Come on, you (expletive), come on, you (expletive), get the (expletive) out of here.'"

At the conclusion of the segment, a smirking Costello said, "You can thank me later."

MSNBC's Erin Burnett, now with CNN, called then-President George W. Bush a "monkey." With videotape rolling of President Bush flanked by French President Nicolas Sarkozy to his left and German Chancellor Angela Merkel to his right, the reporter gushed, "Who could not have a man-crush on that man? I'm not talking about the monkey, either. I'm talking about the other one." The host asked, "Who's the monkey?" Burnett replied, "The monkey in the middle" — meaning President Bush. She, too, later apologized.

The late Tim Russert, in a 2007 interview with The New York Times war correspondent John Burns, repeated an often-cited anti-Iraq War talking point — that Americans expected to be greeted as "liberators" in Iraq, but weren't. Burns, who was in Iraq at the time of the invasion, corrected him: "The American troops were greeted as liberators. We saw it."

Trump is clearly right to fulminate against what he calls the "fake news media." The real question is what took Republicans so long to fight back.

How Long Will NBA Fans Tolerate Trump-Bashing by Head Coaches?

June 1, 2017

The success of NBA San Antonio Spurs coach Gregg Popovich cannot be denied. In his professional career, the Popovich-led Spurs have won five championships. Popovich is also a military vet. Fluent in Russian and armed with an Air Force Academy degree in Soviet studies, his first post was as an intelligence officer assigned to a top-secret facility operating spy satellites. He also played and coached basketball for the Air Force during his five years of active duty, achieving the rank of captain.

So the man is not without experience and insight.

Here's the problem. On several occasions, Popovich has teed off on Donald Trump, the first condemnation taking place just days after Trump's election: "It's still early and I'm still sick to my stomach. Not basically because the Republicans won or anything, but the disgusting tenor and tone and all the comments that have been xenophobic, homophobic, racist, misogynistic, and I live in that country where half the country ignored all that to elect someone. That's the scariest part of the whole thing to me. ... I'm a rich white guy, and I'm sick to my stomach thinking about it. I can't imagine being a Muslim right now, or a woman, or an African-American, a Hispanic, a handicapped person, how disenfranchised they might feel. And for anyone in those groups that voted for him, it's just beyond my comprehension how they ignore all that. And so, my final conclusion is — my big fear is — we are Rome."

That was right after the election. How does Popovich feel now? He recently slammed Trump again:

"Usually things happen in the world and you go to work and you have your family and your friends and you do what you do. To this day, I feel like there's a cloud, a pall over the whole country, in a paranoid, surreal sort of way. It's got nothing to do with the Democrats losing the election; it has to do with the way one individual conducts himself, and that's embarrassing. It's dangerous to our institutions and what we all stand for and what we expect the country to be. For this individual, he's in a game show. Everything that happens begins and ends with him, not our people or our country. Every time he talks about those things, it's a ruse. Disingenuous, cynical."

Imagine what would happen to the career of a coach who said the same thing about, say, President Barack Obama? Couldn't a coach argue that Obama's Iran deal gives the hateful ayatollahs a march toward the acquisition of a nuclear bomb? Couldn't a coach argue that Obama's insistence on releasing detainees from Guantanamo Bay means that a large number of the so-called "worst of the worst" will return to the battlefield, only to kill more Americans or American allies? Couldn't a coach in good faith believe that Obama's failure to use the term "radical Islam" emboldens our enemies and lulls us into a false sense of complacency?

Couldn't a coach argue that Obama, by invoking Ferguson in a United Nations speech and by saying "If I had a son, he'd look like Trayvon," exacerbated racial tensions in America? As for Trump, it should be noted that he got a greater percentage of the black vote and Hispanic vote then did Mitt Romney in 2012, while getting a smaller percentage of the white vote.

Can you imagine the shelf life of any coach who, for example, pointed out that President Obama presided over the worst economic recovery since 1949 and made the case that Obama's tax, spend and regulate policies harmed the economy?

Popovich is not the only publicly anti-Trump coach in the league. Steve Kerr, the coach of the Golden State Warriors, whose father was actually assassinated by Islamic terrorists, criticized President Trump's proposed travel restrictions in January: "I would just say that as someone whose family member was a victim of terrorism ... if we're trying to combat terrorism by banishing people from coming to this country, by really going against the principles of what our country is about and creating fear, it's the wrong way of going about it."

The coach of NBA's Detroit Pistons, Stan Van Gundy, also slammed Trump after his November victory: "I don't think anybody can deny this guy is openly and brazenly racist and misogynistic and ethnic-centric."

The NBA is a private entity, and they could pass a rule banning coaches from making political statements during interviews. The right to make a political statement, of course, does not shield the speaker from the backlash that comes with exercising it.

How much longer will Texas NBA fans tolerate a Trump-bashing coach in a state the President carried by 9 percentage points?

Bill Maher and the 'N-Word'

June 8, 2017

As to Bill Maher's recent use of the N-word on live television, the comedian is probably scratching his head. What exactly are the rules on when, where, how and if the word can be used? Can a non-black, attempting a joke, use the word in public?

On his HBO show, Maher had the following exchange with Nebraska's Republican Sen. Ben Sasse about adults dressing in costumes for Halloween.

Sasse: "It's frowned upon — we don't do that quite as much."

Maher: "I gotta get to Nebraska more."

Sasse: "You're welcome. We'd love to have you work in the fields with us."

Maher: "Work in the fields? Senator, I'm a house n———."

The reaction came fast and hard. Several black celebrities slammed him. Chance the Rapper wants Maher's show canceled, tweeting: "Please HBO Do Not Air Another Episode of Real Time With Bill Maher." Actor Jeffrey Wright tweeted: "'House n———,' eh, Bill Maher? Hi, I'm black twitter. ... When even house n———ship is appropriated, there's pretty much nothing left. And, I mean, who really wants that s——?" He later added: "On an historical note, Bill Maher is the first person ever to think being a 'house n———' is hip."

After HBO criticized Maher's "deeply offensive comment," comedian D.L. Hughley, who uses the N-word in his standup, said: "Now that HBO apologized for Bill Maher saying n———, how about they hire a few? I ain't seen black people on HBO since 'The Wire!'"

Over at MSNBC, the Rev. Al Sharpton said: "There are no exceptions that make this acceptable. Yes, comedians are expected to cross some hard lines. I get it. But let's be clear. Free speech comes with a responsibility to speak up when folks use that word, and that's what I'm doing now. ... You cannot allow anyone to act like there's anything funny in any context about using that word. You have to have one standard, no matter who it is."

Yes, this is same Sharpton who called the then-Mayor of New York City David Dinkins, a black man, a "n———- whore." Sharpton, whom President Donald Trump has called "a con man," rose to fame by championing the cause of Tawana Brawley. This then 15-year-old black New York teen falsely told police that she had been raped and sodomized by a group of white men. One of his associates broke from him and said that Sharpton knew that Brawley was lying. But Sharpton, said the former associate, insisted that fanning this "controversy" would make them "the biggest n———-s in New York." *He* lectures Maher on racial etiquette?

Maher, in using the N-word, is one of many comedians who do so, and not the only non-black. Comedian Jay Mohr uses the word, in standup and on Twitter, and does so without the sort of backlash we're seeing against Maher. To add to the confusion, rapper Kanye West, during a concert, granted white fans their "only opportunity" to use the N-word while singing the lyrics to one of his songs. Black comedians like Redd Foxx, Richard Pryor, Chris Rock, Katt Williams and Kevin Hart have used that word. Today teenagers of all races and both genders consider it hip to call each other the N-word.

HBO, where Maher's show airs, is subscriber-, not advertiser-, based. It airs lots of R-rated movies and other edgy content. So it's akin to paying to see Maher's nightclub act. You expect it to be risque. Complaining about profane language on HBO is like complaining about hearing "Jesus" on "The 700 Club."

Maher has said worse without the furor. In his standup, for example, he called Sarah Palin the C-word and even described her son, who has Down syndrome, as "retarded." He has called her a "dumb t——" — a derisive slang word for female genitalia. On his show, he called Palin and Rep. Michele Bachmann, a Republican tax lawyer who ran for president, "two bimbos."

But "house n———-" is the red line that Maher crossed?

The real problem is the normalizing of the word "n———-." At a mall, I saw two young black boys running. One got ahead of the other. In this mall, whose customers were mostly white, the black kid lagging behind said, "Hey, n———-. Wait up!" I recently received the following letter:

"I am a 60-year-old white man. The other day, I listened to three black men in the neighboring backyard repeatedly using the N-word. The phrase I heard most was, 'that n-word said' or 'that n-word is' or 'that n-word did.' Why does this word qualify as a 'hate crime' if a white person says it when blacks say it all the time?"

Excellent question. Let's ask Sharpton.

If Trump Is 'Liar-In-Chief,' What of Obama's Lies?

June 15, 2017

After the congressional testimony of fired FBI Director James Comey, many Democrats, with notable exceptions, pulled back from the impeachment talk.

MSNBC's Chris Matthews, one of the cheerleaders of the Donald Trump-must-go crowd, even said that Comey failed to make a case for obstruction of justice. "The big story has always been ... the President had something to do with colluding with the Russians. Something to do, a helping hand, encouraging them, feeding their desire, to affect the election in some way, some role they played, some conversation he had with Michael Flynn, or Paul Manafort, or somewhere. And yet what came apart this morning was that theory."

Rep. Maxine Waters, D-Calif., the hyperbolic, rabid Trump-hater, still chanted at an anti-Trump rally on Sunday, "Impeach 45." But she talked less about obstruction and more about Trump's presumed unfitness for office. She called him a "liar."

Liar? Were Waters and the other Democrats who make this claim asleep for the past eight years? Let's talk about just some of the "lies" of the Obama administration.

Barack Obama repeatedly said that his mother, Ann Dunham, fought with insurance carriers to pay her medical and hospital bills as she lay dying from cancer. Obama told this story repeatedly during the 2008 campaign, as well as after he became President, when making the case for Obamacare. After all, if the dastardly insurance companies battle a woman with a PhD and her son with a law degree from Harvard, imagine what insurance carriers will do to you.

During the campaign, Obama said: "She was 52 years old when she died of ovarian cancer, and you know what she was thinking about in the last months of her life? She wasn't thinking about getting well. She wasn't thinking about coming to terms with her own mortality. She had been diagnosed just as she was transitioning between jobs. And she wasn't sure whether insurance was going to cover the medical expenses because they might consider this a pre-existing condition. I remember just being heartbroken, seeing her struggle through the paperwork and the medical bills and the insurance forms." He also said: "For my mother to die of cancer at the age of 53 and have to spend the last months of her life in the hospital room arguing with insurance companies because they're saying that this may be a pre-existing condition and they don't have to pay her treatment, there's something fundamentally wrong about that."

But ex-New York Times reporter Janny Scott wrote a flattering book about Obama's mom. Scott describes Obama's mom's "battle" with insurance carriers quite differently. Scott said Dunham had employer-provided health insurance that "covered most of the costs of her medical treatment. ... The hospital billed her insurance company directly, leaving Ann to pay only the deductible and any uncovered expenses, which, she said, came to several hundred dollars a month." The only quarrel was over a disability policy Dunham had, but her pre-existing condition disqualified her. So much for the mean old insurance company, but Obama's tale helped get Obamacare passed.

Obama, of course, repeatedly said, "If you like your doctor, you can keep your doctor." PolitiFact called it the "Lie of the Year for 2013." PolitiFact wrote, "We found at least 37 times since Obama's inauguration where he or a top administration official made a variation of the pledge that if you like your plan, you can keep it, and we never found an instance in which he offered the caveat that it only applies to plans that hadn't changed after the law's passage. And seven of those 37 cases came after the release of the HHS regulations that defined the 'grandfathering' process, when the impact would be clear."

Obama, who campaigned against the Iraq War, pulled out all the troops against the advice of his entire national security team. But when it became clear that the abrupt pull-out allowed ISIS to metastasize, Obama claimed that he merely followed the timetable for a complete pull-out established by his predecessor. After repeatedly bragging that by puling out he fulfilled a campaign promise, Obama then claimed that President George W. Bush tied his hands.

This brings us to the Iran nuclear deal, Obama's most important foreign-policy decision, which critics claim gives Iran — the No. 1 exporter of terror — a path to a nuclear bomb. The Obama administration claimed that the ruling ayatollahs were divided into two camps, the hardliners and "moderates." Obama's deputy national security adviser for strategic communications, Ben Rhodes, argued that if we want the moderates to prevail, they need this Iran deal to strengthen their political hand. But according to a New York Times writer who profiled Rhodes in 2016: The story of the Iran deal ... was largely manufactured for the purpose for selling the deal. Even where the particulars of that story are true, the implications that readers and viewers are encouraged to take away from those particulars are often misleading or false. ... (This was) the narrative that Rhodes shaped."

To Democrats calling for Trump's head over his "lies," where have you been for the last eight years? Welcome back.

Minimum Wage Laws are Destroying Jobs — Just as Predicted

June 22, 2017

In the '60s my parents opened a small diner near downtown Los Angeles. As a child, I watched my parents sitting at the kitchen table, discussing their plans for what they considered a huge expansion of the business — hiring a dishwasher. But my parents kept putting off the decision, in large part because of a proposed minimum-wage hike. This would've made the additional employee, as I recall my parents concluding, "too expensive."

This brings us to the impact of recent minimum wage hikes in California. The owner of a small restaurant told me that Los Angeles Mayor Eric Garcetti invited several small business owners to city hall to discuss the impact of a proposed minimum wage hike. Several brought profit-and-loss statements. Each business person, the small restaurant owner said, tried to convince the Democratic mayor that their profit margins were too small to take the wage hike without laying people off, cutting hours or raising prices, which usually means a falloff in business.

At the end of the meeting the mayor simply said, "I feel confident that you can absorb the cost."

A new study by two researchers, one with Mathematica Policy Research and the other with Harvard Business School, focused on "the impact of the minimum wage on restaurant closures using data from the San Francisco Bay area." The researchers concluded that "a $1 increase in the minimum wage leads to approximately a 4 to 10 percent increase in the likelihood of exit." They wrote: "The evidence suggests that higher minimum wages increase overall exit rates for restaurants. However, lower quality restaurants, which are already closer to the margin of exit, are disproportionately impacted by increases to the minimum wage." So the most vulnerable restaurants — the more "affordable" ones — appear to be the most hurt by a minimum wage hike.

In January, the East Bay Times reported that 60 restaurants in the San Francisco Bay area had shuttered their doors since September. Even the mighty have fallen. The Fresno Bee recently wrote: "Joining San Francisco's restaurant die-off was rising star AQ, which in 2012 was named a James Beard Award finalist for the best new restaurant in America. The restaurant's profit margins went from a reported 8.5 percent in 2012 to 1.5 percent by 2015. Most restaurants are thought to require margins of 3 and 5 percent."

In San Diego, voters approved an $11.50 per hour minimum wage for 2017, up from an $8 minimum wage in June 2014. This is an increase of 44 percent — in just two and a half years! The San Diego Union Tribune recently reported: "Evidence has emerged of an economic dark side to San Diego's decision last year to vault over the state minimum wage — it may have already destroyed thousands of jobs for low-wage workers even as higher pay helps tens of thousands of others.

"Consider the restaurant industry, for example, which economists study because it relies on low-wage workers, yet generally faces no foreign or out-of-state competition. Amid an abrupt slowdown in growth, nearly 4,000 food-service jobs may have been cut or not created throughout San Diego County from the beginning of 2016 through February of this year."

The now-defunct organization called the Association of Community Organizations for Reform Now came to California years ago to gather signatures on a petition for a ballot measure to increase minimum wage. Incredibly, ACORN sued the state to exempt itself from the then-current minimum wage and overtime laws. In its filings, ACORN said, "The more ACORN must pay each individual outreach worker — either because of minimum wage or overtime requirements — the fewer outreach workers it will be able to hire." Can't make this stuff up.

When George McGovern, the 1972 Democratic presidential candidate, left the Senate, he bought the Stratford Inn, a small Connecticut inn and restaurant. It went bust and he blamed, in part, the very kind regulations he passed as a politician devoid of business experience. "I wish I had known more firsthand about the concerns and problems of American businesspeople while I was a U.S. senator and later a presidential nominee," said McGovern. "... I learned by owning the Stratford Inn is that legislators and government regulators must more carefully consider the economic and management burdens we have been imposing on U.S. businesses. ... Many businesses, especially small independents such as the Stratford Inn, simply can't pass such costs on to their customers and remain competitive or profitable."

As for the mayor of Los Angeles, it should be noted that he worked on a Ph.D.at the London School of Economics. But at this famed institute, Garcetti did not study economics. He studied "ethnicity and nationalism."

Makes sense.

Urban America's Underclass: More Money Won't Solve the Problems

June 22, 2017

PBS NewsHour aired a story last year about Milwaukee, saying many residents call the city "the worst place to be a black man in America." It talked about last year's riots in the city after a cop shot a black man. One black Milwaukee resident explained that this is "what happens when you inflict poverty" on poor black residents. "Inflict poverty"?

In the 50 years following President Lyndon Johnson's launch of the "war on poverty" in 1964, government spent over $22 trillion on welfare and various anti-poverty programs. The problem in our nation's inner cities is *not* a lack of money — it is a moral and spiritual problem largely created by our welfare state. The welfare system encourages women to marry the government and allows men to abandon their financial and moral responsibilities. The problem is fatherlessness.

In a documentary called "Resurrection," rapper Tupac Shakur, who said, "I never knew where my father was or who my father was for sure," actually admitted: "I know for a fact that had I had a father, I'd have some discipline. I'd have more confidence. Your mother cannot calm you down the way a man can. Your mother can't reassure you the way a man can. My mother couldn't show me where my manhood was. You need a man to teach you how to be a man."

In 1995, President Bill Clinton, who pledged to end "welfare as we know it," gave a speech described by a Los Angeles Times writer as "the most sweeping analysis of racial issues of his presidency." On the day of the "March on Washington," Clinton said black men must take more responsibility for their behavior: "Today's march is ... also about black men taking renewed responsibility for themselves, their families and their communities. It's about saying no to crime and drugs and violence. It's about standing up for atonement and reconciliation. It's about insisting that others do the same and offering to help them. It's about the frank admission that unless black men shoulder their load, no one else can help them or their brothers, their sisters and their children escape the hard, bleak lives that too many of them still face. ... It's not racist for whites to assert that the culture of welfare dependency, out-of-wedlock pregnancy and absent fatherhood cannot be broken by social programs, unless there is first more personal responsibility."

In my book, "The Ten Things You Can't Say In America," I wrote about a wealthy, idealistic Philadelphia philanthropist. Committed, concerned and worried about the future of urban — primarily black — kids, he "adopted" 112 inner-city sixth-graders, most of whom were products of broken homes. He promised these students that if they met minimal requirements, including graduating from high school and not getting pregnant or impregnating somebody — he'd pay for all their education, including college tuition.

He provided tutors, workshops, after-school programs and summer programs, as well as counselors to be available when trouble arose, whether personal or otherwise.

Thirteen years later, the Philadelphia Inquirer followed up on the 112 kids and analyzed the results. The percentage of kids going to college was no greater than percentage of kids from similar backgrounds without prepaid educations. The money was wasted.

Forty-five never made it through high school. Of these, 35 dropped out, one died while in school, four died after dropping out, four were working on a GED and one graduated from trade school.

Of the high school graduates, 13 were four-year college graduates, 11 were enrolled in four-year college, five were enrolled in two-year college, 12 had dropped out of two- and four-year colleges, seven graduated trade school, eight were enrolled in trade school, six dropped out of trade school and five got no further education.

Of the 67 boys, 19 grew into adult felons. Among the 45 girls, they had 63 children, and more than half had babies before age 18.

What do we make of this? The answer is simple: It's not about money. It's about values. It's about discipline and application. It's about character — about working hard when you don't want to. And these values are instilled in the home.

The first step is the truth.

As long as blacks feel and act oppressed, as if they are under siege and behind enemy lines, little will change. The formula is simple, but it requires effort: hard work wins; you get out of life what you put into it; you cannot control the outcome, but you are 100 percent in control of the effort. Go to school, study, work hard, arrive early, stay late, pay attention to detail and be honest. That is the best "anti-poverty program" ever conceived.

Trump's 'Divisive' Tweets — More Left-Wing Hypocrisy

July 6, 2017

Critics hammered President Donald Trump for his "sexist" tweet in which he made fun of MSNBC's "Morning Joe" co-host Mika Brzezinski. Trump tweeted: "I heard poorly rated MorningJoe speaks badly of me (don't watch anymore). Then how come low I.Q. Crazy Mika, along with Psycho Joe, came to Mar-a-Lago 3 nights in a row around New Year's Eve, and insisted on joining me. She was bleeding badly from a face-lift. I said no!"

What did the morning show do to incur the President's wrath?

During recent shows, host Joe Scarborough, a former Republican member of Congress, called Trump "the greatest liar that's ever sat in the White House." He said: "I mean, to compare (former President Richard) Nixon to this guy is absolutely ridiculous. He lies every day. A lot of times he lies every minute. He forgets the lie that he told five minutes ago." He also said: "Nobody's saying what Donald Trump's doing now is right. In fact we think it's extraordinarily dangerous. Called the media enemy of the people. It's Stalinist."

Trump, not amused, sent out the "sexist" tweet.

House Minority Leader Nancy Pelosi, D-Calif., among other Democratic leaders, denounced Trump's tweet as sexist, demeaning and divisive. Pelosi, in 2014, actually said, "We never treated President Bush the way they treat President Obama." Maligning Republicans as stupid, racist fascists is so common that Democrats have probably numbed themselves to it.

About Ronald Reagan, Coretta Scott King said, "I am scared that if Ronald Reagan gets into office, we are going to see more of the Ku Klux Klan and a resurgence of the Nazi Party."

Rep. William Clay, D-Mo., said Reagan was "trying to replace the Bill of Rights with fascist precepts lifted verbatim from Mein Kampf."

Esquire magazine writer Harry Stein compared Reagan voters to the "good Germans" in "Hitler's Germany."

Justin Kaplan, the editor of "Bartlett's Familiar Quotations," said about Reagan (who was re-elected, 49 states to one), "I'm not going to disguise the fact that I despise Ronald Reagan."

About President George Herbert Walker Bush, Rep. Maxine Waters, D-Calif., said, "I would like to ... say ... very clearly that I believe George (H.W.) Bush is a racist."

And, in 1994, when Republicans took control of the House, Rep. Charlie Rangel, D-N.Y., said, "It's not 'spic' or 'n———' any more. (Instead Republicans) say 'let's cut taxes.'"

About President George W. Bush, then-Sen. Hillary Clinton, in July 2005, said, "I sometimes feel that Alfred E. Neuman is in charge in Washington," comparing President George W. Bush to Mad magazine's goofball icon.

2004 Democratic presidential candidate John Kerry, on election night, said, "I can't believe I'm losing to this idiot." Earlier that year, when informed that Bush just had an accident on his bicycle, Kerry said, "Did the training wheels come off?"

Feminist attorney Gloria Allred, in 2001, referred to President-elect George W. Bush's possible appointments to his new administration, Colin Powell and Condoleezza Rice, as "Uncle Tom-types."

Unimpressed with the blacks Bush had in his Cabinet, entertainer/activist Harry Belafonte, in August 2005, said, "Hitler had a lot of Jews high up in the hierarchy of the Third Reich."

Billionaire Democratic contributor George Soros, in November 2003, said: "When I hear Bush say, 'You're either with us or against us,' it reminds me of the Germans. My experiences under Nazi and Soviet rule have sensitized me."

Al Gore, in October of 2005, said, to "control and intimidate" the news media, "every day (President George W. Bush's executive branch) unleash squadrons of digital brownshirts to harass and hector any journalist who is critical of the President."

Democratic then-Senate candidate Claire McCaskill, in September 2006, said, "George (W.) Bush let people die on rooftops in New Orleans because they were poor and because they were black."

Rep Barney Frank, D-Mass., in February 2006, accused George W. Bush of "ethnic cleansing by inaction" through his allegedly slow response to hurricane Katrina and its aftermath.

Sen. Hillary Clinton, in January 2006, said before an audience of blacks, "The House of Representatives has been run ... like a plantation — and you know what I'm talking about."

As for President Trump and the presidential race, time and space do not permit even an abbreviated list of the near-pathological attacks. Here are just two. A 2015 column in GQ magazine on Ben Carson, now a member of Trump's Cabinet, was literally entitled, "F—- Ben Carson," using the actual four-letter expletive in the title. Howard Dean, former chair of the DNC, flat-out said, "(Steve Bannon's) a Nazi," referring to the top Trump adviser.

Let's remember that Bill Clinton, not Trump, tried to get Ted Kennedy to support Hillary in 2008 by saying, "A few years ago, this guy (Obama) would have been getting us coffee." Democratic leader Sen. Harry Reid, D-Nev., not Trump, said then-presidential candidate Obama could succeed because he was a "light-skinned" black "with no Negro dialect, unless he wanted to have one."

'Kerosene' Maxine Waters: How Much Longer Will Her District Tolerate Her?

July 13, 2017

Rep. Maxine Waters, D-Calif., has become President Donald Trump's fiercest congressional critic. In eight years, Obama never had a Republican nemesis the likes of Waters, who recently said, "I'm taking the gloves off." Seventeen years ago, I wrote Waters a letter. She never answered. It read, in part:

Congresswoman Waters,

Your power in America, and especially in the black community, is substantial. I honestly, and sincerely, urge you to rethink your positions on several issues. Despite my acknowledged harsh criticisms of you, I never once attacked you personally. I said, on many occasions: "I don't question her heart, but I question her head." I called you a hardworking, tireless warrior for your views.

However, your position on major issues affecting the black community is simply flat-out wrong. Not only do your positions fail to advance the interests of blacks but also, in many cases, actually hurt them.

In "America in Black and White," authors Stephen and Abigail Thernstrom clearly show that the black middle class preceded affirmative action. By affirmative action, I mean preferences, the lowering of standards to achieve "diversity" or "multiculturalism" or "inclusion." I do not include outreach, or using efforts to inform others, irrespective of race, gender, etc., of available opportunities. Moreover, affirmative action insults the hardworking black men and women of this country who, since slavery, built the black middle class, day by day, brick by brick, backache by backache.

In 1963, Ebony magazine ran a series of motivational articles called, "If I Were Young Today." Each month, they asked a black achiever — Federal District Judge Herman Moore, union leader A. Philip Randolph, famed Los Angeles architect Paul Williams — to provide advice to today's youth. Each spoke of drive, vision, hard work and preparation. Not one even implied the need or desire for preferential treatment.

In 1963, Whitney Young, then head of the Urban League, proposed a kind of "Marshall Plan" for blacks. One league member, however, objected to what he called "the heart of it — the business of employing Negroes (because they are Negroes)." Moreover, Whitney Young suggested his "Marshall Plan" for a period of 10 years. This means, if Young prevailed, affirmative action would have ended in 1973!

Lower college-graduation rates for blacks result from lower standards used in minority admissions to achieve campus "diversity." This mismatching of students, placing someone in a major-league school when he or she would have performed better in a triple-A league, causes — according to one study — a loss of $5.3 billion a year to the black community. Moreover, affirmative action in higher education masked the real problem: substandard education in K-12. Yet you resist many changes urban parents want, including vouchers.

You also fight any attempt to roll back the welfare state. Census records from 100 years ago found blacks, in some cases, more likely than whites to marry and have children within a traditional family structure. As recently as 1960, 22 percent of black children were born to unwed parents. Today, the figure stands at 70 percent, with 80 percent spending at least some time living without a father in the house, at least for part of their lives. Racism? Blame Lyndon Johnson's "War on Poverty," coupled with a "you-owe-me" victicrat mindset that creates dependency and fosters irresponsibility.

The majority of blacks reflect increased prosperity, growing homeownership and steady asset accumulation. The minority, the so-called black underclass, remains disturbing. Quite simply, we see too many children having children. It stands, far and away, as America's No. 1 problem. Whatever role racism played, the complete abolition of white racism would leave these problems unresolved.

Racism no longer remains a potent threat in American life. Hard work, personal responsibility, focus, avoiding slovenly behavior and getting an education will create growth and opportunity. You display precisely these qualities in your life and career, and they formed the basis for your success.

But you refuse to acknowledge this good news, preferring to blame racism. In 1973, former Black Panther Joanne Chesimard gunned down a New Jersey State Highway Patrol officer. A jury convicted her of murder and sentenced her to life in prison. In a daring breakout, Chesimard escaped from prison and fled to Cuba. Congress passed a unanimous resolution urging Castro to send Chesimard back to America and face charges. You, however, wrote Castro a letter, urging him to let her stay, stating she was persecuted for her political beliefs and affiliations. You further likened her to Martin Luther King!

The letter went on from there.

For the 2018 midterm election, Waters has a Republican challenger. His name is Omar Navarro, born and raised in her district, one that is now 46 percent Hispanic and 24 percent black. Navarro ran against her the last election cycle, getting only 24 percent of the vote. But that was before Waters became the "face of the resistance." Some tacticians argue that with Waters leading the "Trump Is Public Enemy No. 1" brigade, the Republican Party is better off. Perhaps so.

But what about America?

Collusion? What About Chinagate and Ted Kennedy's Outreach to the USSR?

July 20, 2017

During President Bill Clinton's 1996 campaign for re-election, several individuals allegedly worked on behalf of the Chinese government to influence the presidential election in favor of Clinton.

"Chinagate" began when the Los Angeles Times reported, a couple months before the '96 election, the following:

"The Democratic National Committee has returned a $250,000 contribution from a recently established subsidiary of a South Korean electronics company because it violated a ban on donations from foreign nationals in U.S. elections, a party spokesman said Friday. ...

"David Eichenbaum, DNC communications director ... said that the DNC fund-raiser who was responsible for the contribution was under the impression, erroneously as it turned out, that it fulfilled the legal qualifications. He said it was unclear whether the fund-raiser was misled or there had been a misunderstanding."

DNC did the standard "Oops, we made a boo-boo, here's your money back, it's all OK now" dog and pony show. That worked for a while. But a few months later, on Feb. 13, 1997, The Washington Post's Bob Woodward and Brian Duffy reported:

"A Justice Department investigation into improper political fund-raising activities has uncovered evidence that representatives of the People's Republic of China sought to direct contributions from foreign sources to the Democratic National Committee before the

1996 presidential campaign, officials familiar with the inquiry said.
...

"The Chinese effort to win influence with the Clinton administration can be traced to 1993, one source said. ... Some investigators suspected a Chinese connection to the current fund-raising scandal because several DNC contributors and major fund-raisers had ties to Beijing. Last February, Charles Yah Lin Trie, a fund-raiser for the Democratic National Committee, used his influence with party officials to bring Wang Jun, head of a weapons trading company owned by the Chinese military, to a White House coffee with Clinton.

"Wang also heads a prominent, state-owned investment conglomerate. Clinton has since said he should not have met with Wang, and $640,000 in checks that Trie delivered to president's legal defense fund has been returned because of questions about the source of the funds."

The DNC vice chairman and fundraiser at the center of the DNC's illegal contribution was formerly a top executive involved with Asian and Chinese corporations, with some holdings sold to the Chinese government. Before joining the DNC, he left his corporate job with a large severance and worked at the Commerce Department for 18 months, where he enjoyed a top-secret clearance. Evidence showed more than 70 calls from his Commerce office to a bank controlled by his former corporation; memos of calls from Chinese embassy officials; three meetings scheduled with Chinese government officials; a breakfast and a dinner at the Chinese embassy; and at least one visit to the "residence of the Chinese ambassador."

After a year of investigation, FBI director Louis Freeh sent Clinton Attorney General Janet Reno a 22-page memorandum, stating, "It is difficult to imagine a more compelling situation for appointing an independent counsel."

Several months later, Charles LaBella, head of the Justice Department's campaign-finance task force, also sent a report to Reno recommending she appoint an independent counsel. The evidence, LaBella said, "suggests a level of knowledge within the White House — including the president's and first lady's offices — concerning the injection of foreign funds into the reelection effort."

He also said, "If these allegations involved anyone other than the president, vice president, senior White House or DNC and Clinton/Gore '96 officials, an appropriate investigation would have commenced months ago without hesitation."

Reno, however, declined all requests for an independent counsel. Before Chinagate, Sen. Ted Kennedy, thinking of running for president in 1988, reportedly offered to *help the Soviets* influence the 1984 election. Desperate to stop President Ronald Reagan's re-election, Kennedy, as first reported in The London Times in 1992, reached out via an intermediary to the Soviet KGB.

The London Times revealed a 1983 KGB document from KGB chief Viktor Chebrikov to the then-leader of the USSR, Yuri Andropov. Chebrikov relayed an offer presented to the Soviet leaders from Kennedy, delivered in person by "Sen. Edward Kennedy's close friend and trusted confidant" John Tunney, a former Democratic senator who was Kennedy's law school roommate.

Kennedy, according to the memo, offered to help the Soviets deal with Reagan, whom Kennedy perceived as a warmonger. Kennedy would "arm Soviet officials with explanations regarding problems of nuclear disarmament so they may be better prepared and more convincing during appearances in the USA." In exchange, Kennedy wanted Soviet aid in challenging Reagan's re-election. Kennedy offered to use his influential friends in liberal American media to arrange television interviews for Andropov. This would soften the Soviets' image, Kennedy suggested, and help brand Reagan as reckless and dangerous.

The memo said, "Kennedy does not discount that during the 1984 campaign, the Democratic Party may officially turn to him to lead the fight against the Republicans and elect their candidate president."

To summarize, there was no special prosecutor for Chinagate. And few in the media followed up on the Kennedy/KGB story when it broke. This explains why Trump supporters, despite the selective hyperventilation over Russian "collusion," still back their man.

It's High Noon on the GOP's Promise to 'Repeal and Replace'

July 27, 2017

The reason Republicans can't "come together" on a repeal-and-replacement plan for Obamacare is that the American people haven't come together on what they want.

True, polls show Obamacare remains unpopular. But the various Republican replacement proposals have polled even worse. And when you break down the answers, Obamacare is unpopular-ish. Americans, for example, like the idea of preventing insurance carriers from denying coverage to people who have pre-existing conditions. Similarly, polls show that Americans like compelling an insurance company to keep a child on a parent's policy until the child is 26 years old. Americans wish to prevent insurance carriers from "discriminating" on price based on their projections of who is more likely to use health care.

When asked whether they believe "health care is a right," many polls find that a majority of Americans say yes. Once again, Obamacare was designed to continue the march toward a Canadian-style, single-payer health care system — a type of cradle-to-grave "Medicare for all." Under so-called single-payer, the federal government becomes the insurer, eradicating private health care insurance. So "single-payer" means that every American taxpayer is paying for the insurance — and all the overhead costs of a bloated, inefficient, bureaucratic federal government that faces no competition or incentive to be cost-efficient.

Former Democratic National Committee Chairman Howard Dean, an early advocate of the single-payer system, later said he supported the "public option" — a federal Medicare-type insurance available for purchase. It would coexist in the marketplace with private insurance, theoretically offering the consumer a "choice" between private or government insurance.

During the 2008 presidential campaign, Dean talked about the health care proposals of Democratic candidates Barack Obama and then-Sen. Hillary Clinton: "I think while someday we may end up with a single-payer system, it's clear that we're not going to do it all at once, so I think both candidates' health care plans are a big step forward."

In other words, Obamacare was just a steppingstone along the path. The end game is the single-payer system. Obamacare was intended to fail, given the Democrats' real goal of a Canadian-style taxpayer-paid health care. Harry Reid openly said so. The Las Vegas Sun reported in 2013:

"(Senate Majority Leader Harry) Reid said he thinks the country has to 'work our way past' insurance-based health care during a Friday night appearance on Vegas PBS' program 'Nevada Week in Review.'

"'What we've done with Obamacare is have a step in the right direction, but we're far from having something that's going to work forever,' Reid said.

"When then asked by panelist Steve Sebelius whether he meant ultimately the country would have to have a health care system that abandoned insurance as the means of accessing it, Reid said: 'Yes, yes. Absolutely, yes.'"

Barack Obama, then a state senator from Illinois, said: "I happen to be a proponent of a single-payer, universal health care program. I see no reason why the United States of America, the wealthiest country in the history of the world, spending 14 percent of its gross national product on health care, cannot provide basic health insurance to everybody. ... A single-payer health care plan, a universal health care plan. That's what I'd like to see. But as all of you know, we may not get there immediately. Because first we've got to take back the White House, we've got to take back the Senate, and we've got to take back the House." And later, then-President

Obama reiterated his stance, with the qualification that if starting "from scratch" he'd have a single-payer system.

Never mind that Claude Castonguay, the "father of Quebec Medicare," criticized his own invention, and said that the mistake was not encouraging more private-sector participation. In the '60s, Castonguay chaired a Canadian government committee on health care reform. He urged Quebec, his home province, to enact government-administered health care, paid for by all tax levies on its citizens. Quebec obliged.

Eventually the rest of Canada followed suit. But 40 years later Castonguay, serving as chairman of a government committee reviewing Quebec health care in 2008, said the system was in "crisis."

"We thought we could resolve the system's problems by rationing services or injecting massive amounts of new money into it," said Castonguay. "We are proposing to give a greater role to the private sector so that people can exercise freedom of choice." His recommendations included contracting out services to the private sector, instating co-pays to see doctors and legalizing private health care insurance. Radical stuff.

Never mind that, a year later, the newly elected president of the Canadian Medical Association said that her country's health care system was "imploding" and said, "We all agree that things are more precarious than perhaps Canadians realize." At the same time, the CMA's outgoing president said, "A health care revolution has passed us by" and "competition should be welcomed, not feared." Better late to Economics 101 than never.

The GOP took a big step this week toward fulfilling its promise to repeal and replace Obamacare by passing a procedural vote to debate the issue in the Senate.

Now comes the hard part.

Trump? What About the 'Chaos' in the Clinton White House?

August 3, 2017

In a newspaper piece about a White House in turmoil, a prominent paper described an atmosphere of beleaguered aides confused by their unscripted boss, a man who needed a "rudder on what many believed was a loose and listing ship."

This is not from a recent piece about President Donald Trump's White House. The Washington Post, in 1997, wrote this about President Bill Clinton and the state of his presidency in mid-1994. The White House staff, wrote the Post, "was suffering from what increasingly looked to be callowness and naivete." Enter veteran congressman and new chief of staff Leon Panetta, who learned, as he put it, that "no one had an organizational chart." He added, "As far as I know, anybody who walked down the hall walked in (to the Oval Office)." Clinton, whose approval ratings were at one time about as bad as Trump's, went on to an easy re-election.

As to Trump's changing of White House personnel, President Barack Obama, over his two terms, had five chiefs of staff. One "interim" chief of staff lasted less time than did Reince Priebus. Bill Clinton and Ronald Reagan, two-term presidents, had four each.

Obama had four secretaries of Defense, more than Clinton and Reagan. In the case of Obama's first three, upon departure, they had significant policy differences with the boss.

Leon Panetta, Obama's second secretary of Defense, complained about what he considered Obama's poor leadership, one that "avoids the battle, complains and misses opportunities." On Iraq, Panetta felt that Obama "kind of lost his way" when he pulled out all the troops over Panetta's objection.

Obama declared a "red line" in Syria, that the U.S. would strike if Syria used chemical weapons. Panetta criticized Obama's flip-flop, which left the decision to Congress, which, Panetta says, was, "as he well knew, an almost certain way to scotch any action." This hurt America's credibility, Panetta said, because "the power of the United States rests on its word, and clear signals are important both to deter adventurism and to reassure allies that we can be counted on."

On Obama's deliberation over whether to intervene in Libya, Robert Gates, his first secretary of Defense, a holdover from the George W. Bush administration, wrote: "I was running out of patience on multiple fronts, but most of all people blithely talking about the use of military force as though it were some kind of video game." White House staff, said Gates, were "talking about military options with the President without Defense being involved."

He even said that Hillary Clinton and Obama both admitted that when they were in the Senate and opposed the Iraq "surge," they did so for political, not technical, reasons. Gates was shocked that they so candidly admitted it during a meeting he attended: "Hillary told the president that her opposition to the (2007) surge in Iraq had been political because she was facing him in the Iowa primary. ... The President conceded vaguely that opposition to the Iraq surge had been political. To hear the two of them making these admissions, and in front of me, was as surprising as it was dismaying."

Gates dismissed the then-pending Iran nuclear deal as a "hope" that Gates called "unrealistic": "The pursuit of the agreement is based on the President's hope that over a 10-year period with the sanctions being lifted that the Iranians will become a constructive stakeholder. ... That as their economy begins to grow again ... they will abandon their ideology, their theology, their revolutionary principles, their meddling in various parts of the region. And frankly, I believe that's very unrealistic."

Speaking of dysfunction, Obama's secretary of Defense No. 3, Chuck Hagel, said the Obama White House tried to "destroy" him even after he submitted his resignation, with some administration officials maligning him in anonymous comments to the media during his last days in office. "I don't know what the purpose was," he said. "To this day, I'm still mystified by that." Hagel reportedly battled the White House's micromanaging of the Pentagon. He claimed the chairman of the Joint Chiefs complained, "White House staffers were calling generals 'and asking fifth-level questions that the White House should not be involved in.'" These were serious criticisms by ex-secretaries of Defense about an incumbent president during wartime. Yet the media did not foam at the mouth.

This is not to say that there haven't been missteps, pullbacks and recalibrations at a dizzying rate in Trump's new administration. This stems from the top, and the recent personnel changes make it clear that Trump *knows* he needs discipline. Business and politics are two different creatures, as a frustrated President Trump has, no doubt, discovered. Building an ice rink in Central Park under budget and ahead of schedule is one thing. Getting a consensus on political issues like "repeal and replace" is quite another.

But few remember the tumult of the early Clinton months. If Trump succeeds in getting the economy humming at about 3 percent growth, the musical chairs of today will be a distant memory.

The Shameful Blackout of Thomas, Sowell and Williams

August 10, 2017

Clarence Thomas, one of nine members of the Supreme Court and the second black to ever join the Court, is not in the National Museum of African American History and Culture in Washington, D.C. Asked to explain Thomas' absence, the chief spokeswoman for the Smithsonian said, "The museum's exhibitions are based on themes, not individuals."

Yet the museum plans to add a popular local D.C. television news broadcaster. The museum's founding director, Lonnie Bunch, said the broadcaster "symbolized that it was really important that America was changing and his presence was a symbol of that change." And Thomas, raised in poverty to become only the second black to sit on the Supreme Court, is *not* "a symbol of that change"?

Left-wing blacks — and that's the overwhelming majority — feel that black conservatives like *damage* the black community. Never mind that most Clarence Thomas-haters could not identify a single case Thomas decided with which they disagree.

One line of attack against Thomas goes as follows. Thomas "took advantage" of race-based preferences to get into college and law school, but then "turned his back on those behind" by arguing that such preferences violate the 14th Amendment.

What these critics assert is that but for race-based preferences, Clarence Thomas would likely be working the deep-fryer at McDonald's. Assume, for the moment, that but for race-based preferences, Thomas would not have gotten into the particular schools he attended, College of the Holy Cross in Worcester, Massachusetts, and Yale Law School. But in America thousands of colleges and universities, from community colleges to Harvard, accept students of varying abilities with financial assistance readily available. Surely the driven, hardworking, academically oriented Clarence Thomas could have and would have found admission into schools matching his skills and ability.

Here's another problem with race-based preferences. Studies document a disproportionately high college-dropout rate for minority students admitted with lower test scores and grades than their peers selected without preferences. How is this mismatching of value to the "beneficiary" if it leads to a higher dropout rate, with the frustrated student giving up and leaving school in debt? The student often blames his failure to succeed at this high level on unfair, if not racist, professors.

The African-American Museum's discrimination against Thomas provides just one example of the black anti-conservative bigotry. Here's another. Every year, the black monthly magazine Ebony lists its "Power 100," defined as those "who lead, inspire and demonstrate through their individual talents, the very best in Black America." Each year Thomas is conspicuously absent. Apparently, as a sitting black justice on the Supreme Court of the United States, Thomas does not "lead, inspire and demonstrate ... the very best in Black America."

Ebony not only excludes Clarence Thomas but also shuts out prominent conservatives Thomas Sowell and Walter Williams.

As for Sowell, he's only an economist and writer whom playwright David Mamet once called "our greatest contemporary philosopher." Sowell, who never knew his father, was raised by a great-aunt and her two grown daughters. They lived in Harlem, where he was the first in his family to make it past the sixth grade. He left home at 17, served as a Marine in the Korean War, graduated magna cum laude from Harvard, earned a master's degree at Columbia University the next year, followed by a Ph.D. in economics at the University of Chicago.

Sowell, at 87, authored some four dozen books (not counting revised editions) and wrote hundreds of scholarly articles and essays in periodicals and thousands of newspaper columns. In 2015, Forbes magazine said: "It's a scandal that economist Thomas Sowell has not been awarded the Nobel Prize. No one alive has turned out so many insightful, richly researched books." Yet, thanks in part to the Ebony shutout, many blacks have never heard of him.

How does Ebony justify excluding economist and writer Walter Williams, former chairman of the economics department of George Mason University, where he still teaches? Raised by a single mother, he lived in Philadelphia's Richard Allen housing projects. He served as a private in the Army before earning a bachelor's degree at a state university, followed by a master's and a Ph.D. in economics at UCLA. Williams has written a dozen books on economics and race, including the inspirational "Up From the Projects: An Autobiography," and was recently the subject of a documentary about his life.

The exclusion of people like Clarence Thomas, Thomas Sowell and Walter Williams explains why there's no serious discussion in the black community about government dependency; school choice; the damage done by high taxes, excessive regulation and laws like minimum wage; and why blacks should rethink their allegiance to the Democratic Party.

Charlottesville: David Duke
Still Matters — Who Knew?

August 17, 2017

Who knew David Duke mattered?

Cable news made the former wizard of the KKK quite visible in Charlottesville, at what planners billed as the largest gathering of the "alt-right community." The "Unite the Right" rally encouraged the like-minded to go to and demonstrate in Charlottesville, Virginia. Counter-protesters, of course, showed up, and many violent clashes ensued. When the dust settled, a woman had been killed and 19 injured when a suspect apparently intentionally drove his car into a crowd of people, although the matter remains under investigation. Two police officers died when their patrol helicopter crashed.

Duke got considerable airtime in Charlottesville. Never mind that the last time he was taken even remotely seriously was in 1991 when he ran for governor of Louisiana. Not a single Republican congressional lawmaker supported him. Mary Matalin, chief of staff of the Republican National Committee, said: "He is not a Republican. We never considered him a Republican. There will be no involvement in his campaign whatsoever." He lost by a large margin. He sought office four more times, losing each race. He also served time for mail fraud and tax evasion.

President George Herbert Walker Bush issued this scathing dismissal: "When someone asserts the Holocaust never took place, then I don't believe that person ever deserves one iota of public trust. When someone has so recently endorsed Nazism, it is inconceivable that someone can reasonably aspire to a leadership role in a free society."

Were it not for cable news digging Duke up from time to time, he'd probably be working road construction under an assumed name in Kalamazoo.

Can we agree to denounce all bigots — whether a David Duke or Maxine Waters or Rev. Al Sharpton? After all, Waters called President Donald Trump's cabinet members "scumbags" and said, "I've never seen anybody as disgusting or as disrespectful as he is." She recently even called Democrat Alan Dershowitz a "racist."

As for Sharpton, he has a long list of racist, homophobic and anti-Semitic comments that in a rational world would long ago have consigned him to the ash bin of history. This is the man who, among many outrages over his career as a "civil rights activist," falsely accused a white man of raping a black teenager and to this day has never apologized. He helped to incite three days of anti-Semitic rioting in Crown Heights, New York, a tragedy that one Columbia University professor called "a modern-day pogrom." Yet this bigot who whipped up the Crown Heights atmosphere by bellowing, "If the Jews want to get it on, tell them to pin their yarmulkes back and come over to my house," somehow visited the Obama White House, according to The Washington Post, 72 times during Obama's first six years.

But it's Trump aide Steven Bannon whom Trump critics malign as an "anti-Semite."

After the violence in Charlottesville, Trump issued a statement denouncing "hatred, bigotry and violence on many sides." But he got hammered for "not calling out" the white nationalist groups by name and for assigning blame to both sides. Critics accused Trump of making a "moral equivalence" — equating white nationalists and Nazi sympathizers to those who oppose them. Normal people thought he meant both sides of the people fighting in the streets. But Trump's critics accused him of equating Nazis with anti-Nazis — or something like that. So he issued another statement.

Trump said: "Racism is evil. And those who cause violence in its name are criminals and thugs, including the KKK, neo-Nazis, white supremacists and other hate groups that are repugnant to everything we hold dear as Americans."

Critics then called it too little, too late, especially coming from the man they consider the bigot in chief. Had Trump called out the bad guys by name, critics would've blasted him for not giving out their Social Security numbers, too.

The bigot in the White House actually got a *smaller* share of the white vote than did Mitt Romney in 2012, while getting a *larger* percentage of the black, Hispanic and Asian votes than Romney did. Apparently blacks, Hispanics and Asians are too stupid to realize that they voted for a man who, right in front of them, reached out to people who hate them. Apparently, the white racists that Trump reached out to are too stupid to realize they've attached themselves to a guy who is attracting the very people that white racists hate — people of color.

Two related "race" themes, fervently believed by the left, drive this hatred for Trump. First, the left believes, despite overwhelming evidence to the contrary, that whites' anti-black racism remains a major problem — even after America became the only predominantly white country in the world to elect a black person to lead it. Second, they believe that Trump won by catering to white racists. Neither is true. But the left's desire to embrace these two narratives is, to them, much like climate change. It's settled science.

Why Stop at Reassessing Confederate Monuments? What About the Kennedy Brothers?

August 24, 2017

As we rewrite history and remove Confederate monuments deemed "offensive" when viewed through the prism of contemporary standards of morality, reasonable people ask: Where does one draw the line? The left, for example, reveres the Kennedy brothers, John, Robert and Edward. But if evaluated by today's standards of social justice, would these left-wing icons hold up?

In Sen. Ted Kennedy's case, how does the monument-removing left feel about the kiss Kennedy blew Gov. George Wallace a mere 10 years after Wallace delivered what became perhaps that era's most infamous defense of segregation? At Wallace's request, Kennedy spoke in Alabama at a 1973 Fourth of July "Spirit of America" rally honoring Wallace in 1973.

Just 10 years earlier, Wallace defended "Jim Crow," or legal segregation, by shouting, "Segregation now, segregation tomorrow, segregation forever," and attempted to prevent blacks from attending the University of Alabama by blocking a campus doorway. Yet at this July 1973 rally, where Wallace received a "Patriotism Award," guest speaker Kennedy praised Wallace as a believer in the "true spirit of America," who supported the right of everyone to "speak his mind and be heard." Kennedy also talked about the things the two men had in common, including that they "don't corrupt," "don't malign" and "don't abuse" the people's trust.

John F. Kennedy won a razor-thin race in 1960. The black vote was crucial. Just four years earlier, nearly 40 percent of blacks voted Republican. Kennedy got 68 percent of the black vote, thanks in part to the tireless efforts of entertainer Sammy Davis Jr. The brilliant singer/actor/dancer/musician/comedian Davis campaigned hard for Kennedy, and even postponed his wedding to a white actress until after the election to avoid costing votes from those who disapproved of interracial marriages. But after Kennedy got elected, and Davis then got married, the President-elect disinvited him from performing at Kennedy's inaugural gala. It got worse. Twentieth Century Fox, to which Sammy's new wife was under contract, invoked the morals clause and let her go, effectively ending her career.

The NAACP criticized Ted Kennedy's appearance at the Wallace rally, and during Jack Kennedy's presidency civil rights groups grew frustrated over Kennedy's failure to offer a civil rights bill. But JFK, afraid of alienating the South, wanted to delay any legislation until after the 1964 re-election.

This brings us to Robert Kennedy. FBI head J. Edgar Hoover sought and received permission to wiretap Dr. Martin Luther King Jr. The person granting him permission? Attorney General Robert F. Kennedy.

Some historians argue that Kennedy agreed to the wiretap because he feared Hoover possessed scandalous files on the Kennedy brothers. But other historians say Robert Kennedy sincerely believed, as Hoover did, that communists infiltrated King's civil rights team.

"I asked the FBI to make an intensive investigation of Martin Luther King," Robert Kennedy later told journalist Anthony Lewis. "We never wanted to get close to him just because of these contacts and connections that he had, which we felt were damaging to the civil rights movement and because we were so intimately involved in the struggle for civil rights, it also damaged us."

Never mind that FBI documents later released do, indeed, show that a close King adviser also served as a high-level operative and financier of the Communist Party USA. Tell this to today's social justice warriors in Philadelphia where, for example, locals debate whether to move a statue of a mayor whom some black

Philadelphians call racist. Whatever Mayor Frank Rizzo was and did, he didn't own slaves.

Is removing Confederate statues a priority issue among blacks, the group presumably most offended by the monuments? Not really. A new NPR/PBS NewsHour/Marist poll shows that more blacks want the monuments to stay than want them removed — 44 percent to 40 percent, respectively. Add in the 16 percent who are "unsure" and a majority of blacks either want the statues to stay or don't seem to care much one way or the other. Also, if Confederate statues inflict such misery on the psyche of blacks, why do tests repeatedly show that blacks have *higher* self-esteem than whites?

Charles Barkley, the ex-basketball star turned television analyst, said he's "always ignored" Confederate statues. He said: "I'm 54 years old. I've never thought about those statues a day in my life. I think if you ask most black people, to be honest, they ain't thought a day in their life about those stupid statues. ... What we as black people need to do ... we need to worry about getting our education. We need to stop killing each other. We need to try to find a way to have more economic opportunity. Those things are important and significant."

Barkley makes more sense than many of our so-called leaders. Why don't we first tackle issues like the breakdown of the nuclear family, noncompetitive urban public schools and gang-related violence before we move on to Confederate monuments?

Confederate Monuments: The Problem With Politically Correct History

August 31, 2017

Malcolm X, as a member of the Nation of Islam, preached anti-Semitism and called the white man "devil." After the assassination of John F. Kennedy, Malcolm X dismissed the murder as a case of "the chickens coming home to roost."

In Spike Lee's biographical drama, "Malcolm X," a white teenage girl approaches the angry activist and says, "Excuse me, Mr. X. Hi. I've read some of your speeches, and I honestly believe that a lot of what you have to say is true. And I'm a good person, in spite of what my ancestors did, and I just — I wanted to ask you, what can a white person like myself who isn't prejudiced, what can I do to help you ... further your cause?" He stares sternly, and replies, "Nothing." She leaves in tears.

But Malcolm X changed. He visited Mecca, where he saw people of all colors worshipping together. It changed the way he thought. He repudiated his anger toward whites after discovering that people were more similar than they were different. He renounced the racist ideology of the Nation of Islam, and in doing so knowingly signed his own death warrant. He was assassinated by members of the Nation of Islam.

Alabama Gov. George Wallace, in 1963, proclaimed, "Segregation now, segregation tomorrow, segregation forever," at his inauguration, and later stood in a doorway at the University of Alabama to bar blacks from entering. Nine years later, Wallace took a would-be assassin's bullet, leaving him paralyzed. Older, wiser and chastened by the attempt on his life, Wallace changed. Wallace, one day and without invitation, went to a black church where 300 black clergymen were holding a conference. He asked to speak. Wallace asked for forgiveness. He said to the church leaders, "I never had hate in my heart for any person. But I regret my support of segregation and the pain it caused the black people of our state and nation. ... I've learned what pain is, and I'm sorry if I've caused anybody else pain. Segregation was wrong — and I am sorry."

The voters in Alabama returned the former governor to office, but this time, he received black support and made several black appointments. The damage Wallace did through his actions and rhetoric was profound, and despite the assassination attempt, he lived long enough to undo some of it.

Even a Confederate general can change.

Confederate Gen. William Mahone, one of General Robert E. Lee's most able commanders, owned slaves before the Civil War. But after the war, he led an interracial political movement. He organized and became the leader of the Readjuster Party, the most successful interracial political alliance in the post-emancipation South. In 1881, Mahone was elected to the U.S. Senate, at the time split 37-37 between Republicans and Democrats. But Mahone aligned with the Republicans, the party founded two decades earlier by Northerners trying to stop the expansion of slavery.

From 1879 through 1883, Mahone's Readjuster Party dominated Virginia, with a governor in the statehouse, two Readjusters in the U.S. Senate and Readjusters representing six of the state's 10 congressional districts. Under Mahone's leadership, his coalition also controlled the state legislature, the courts and many of the state's coveted federal offices.

The Readjusters established what became Virginia State University, the first state-supported college to train black teachers. Democrats described the hated Readjusters and Republicans as advocates of "black domination."

What about Lt. Gen. James Longstreet? One of Lee's favorite generals, Longstreet not only became a Republican after the war and served in Republican administrations but also fought against the racist White League in New Orleans.

After the Civil War, Longstreet moved to New Orleans, where he urged Southerners to support the Republican Party and endorsed their candidate, Ulysses S. Grant, for president in 1868. He commanded blacks in the New Orleans Metropolitan Police Force against the anti-Reconstruction White League (a paramilitary arm of the Democratic Party) at the Battle of Liberty Place in 1874. He was shot and held captive for several days. He accepted political appointments from Republicans, and even dared criticize Gen. Lee. For this "betrayal," white Southerners pronounced Longstreet a "scalawag" and "leper of the community."

Where does this viewing of history through the prism of modern-day feelings end? Dr. Martin Luther King Jr. once gave advice to a gay young man that today would be heresy. King suggested he battle his feelings, strongly implying that the young man needed therapy and sexual re-orientation. Today, that kind of advice gets one branded a Neanderthal. President John F. Kennedy, frustrated with a high-profile Democrat who hadn't supported his election, threatened to banish him by giving him an obscure ambassadorship to one of the, as Kennedy put it, "boogie republics" in Africa. Tell that to Black Lives Matter.

Harvey Shows America's Colorblind Spirit — Bad News for Race Hustlers

September 7, 2017

Hurricane Harvey reveals an America that many in the media seem not to know exists: a multi-ethnic, multiracial country where people, for the most part, get along. For those who claim that President Donald Trump "coarsened" our politics and "set back race relations," Hurricane Harvey was pretty bad optics.

Only weeks ago, some Democrats were counting the days toward Trump's impeachment and an early departure from the presidency. But last week they saw Trump, in Texas, looking quite presidential in his role as comforter in chief. They saw photos of a president soothing and embracing survivors, no matter their race or gender or sexual orientation. If he is a germaphobe, his fear must be in remission, as he hugged adult survivors and held kids in his arms. Texans, including black ones, appeared pleased by Trump's visit even as Democrats like Maxine Waters have denounced him as "racist," calling for his impeachment as Harvey was bearing down on Texas.

Imagine this: neighbors helping neighbors, irrespective of race. But really, this is an old American story. Frenchman Alexis de Tocqueville traveled to this fascinating new country called the United States of America in the 1830s. He wrote about what he considered an astonishing number of "mutual aid societies," or charitable organizations and clubs set up to help a community's needy. Tocqueville wrote: "Americans group together to hold fetes, found seminaries, build inns, construct churches, distribute books, dispatch missionaries to the antipodes. They establish hospitals, prisons, schools by the same method. Finally, if they wish to highlight a truth or develop an opinion by the encouragement of a great example, they form an association. ...

"The love and respect of your neighbors must be gained by a long series of small services, hidden deeds of goodness, a persistent habit of kindness, and an established reputation of selflessness. ... I have seen Americans making great and sincere sacrifices for the key common good and a hundred times I have noticed that, when needs be, they almost always gave each other faithful support."

Tocqueville considered Americans' remarkable spirit of charitable giving a matter of enlightened self-interest: "American moralists do not claim that one must sacrifice oneself for one's fellows because it is a fine thing to do but they are bold enough to say that such sacrifices are as necessary to the man who makes them as to those gaining from them. ... They do not, therefore, deny that every man can pursue his own self-interest but they turn themselves inside out to prove that it is in each man's interest to be virtuous. ... Enlightened self-love continually leads them to help one another and inclines them to devote freely a part of their time and wealth to the welfare of the state."

America just elected and re-elected a black president. Still, President Barack Obama famously said racism is "still part of (America's) DNA." Well, America's DNA clearly changed, and dramatically so. In 1958, when Gallup asked whether Americans would vote for a black person for president, 54 percent said, "No." A 2006 Los Angeles Times/Bloomberg poll found just 3 percent of Republicans and 4 percent of Democrats said they would not vote for a black presidential candidate. In fact, more Americans (14 percent) said they would not vote for a Mormon or a 72-year-old than the number who refused to vote for a black president.

In the 1950s, interracial black-white marriages were extremely rare. Today, intermarriage of all races and ethnicities accounts for 17 percent of all marriages. This is why sane observers of O.J. Simpson's 1995 murder trial considered its defense a joke: that LAPD officers, including an Asian-American criminalist, seething at Simpson for having married a blue-eyed blonde, leaped at their opportunity to frame him. In liberal Los Angeles, where intermarriage is common? In the 1950s over 90 percent of Americans disapproved of black-white marriages, while recent polls say about 90 percent approve.

If America were as racist as many in the media think, why do blacks excel in two of the most competitive fields — sports and entertainment? On Forbes' list of highest-earning celebrities, blacks occupy seven of the top 25 slots, including Sean Combs, who clocks in at $130 million annually; Beyonce at $105 million; and Drake at $94 million.

On Forbes' list of highest-earning athletes, blacks occupy 13 of the top 25 spots, including LeBron James at $86 million; Kevin Durant at $60 million; and Stephen Curry at $47 million.

Watch out, Trump-hating media. As more blacks recognize that Republicans are not out to get them, and they look at cities like Detroit under Democratic leadership, Trump can potentially tip the black vote in his party's direction more than any Republican since Abraham Lincoln.

Moving the Goal Post on Racism

September 14, 2017

In 1964, Dr. Martin Luther King Jr. appeared on a BBC news show. The host asked King about Attorney General Robert Kennedy's prediction, an audacious one at the time, that a black man could be elected president in 40 years.

King thought it would not take that long: "There are certain problems and prejudices and mores in our society which make it difficult now. However, I am very optimistic about the future. Frankly, I have seen certain changes in the United States over the last two years that surprise me. ... On the basis of this, I think we may be able to get a Negro president in less than 40 years. I would think that this could come in 25 years or less."

It took 44 years.

The day after the election of President Barack Obama front-page stories in newspapers all over the country, including The New York Times, quoted black parents saying things like, "For the first time in my life I can truly look my child in the eye and say, yes, you could become president someday."

A tearful Jesse Jackson said he never thought he would see the day. Rep. John Lewis, D-Ga., a civil rights leader who marched with Dr. King, said: "I feel very grateful that I'm still here to be here during this unbelievable historic moment in our country. This is a day of thanksgiving, a night of celebration. ... It's unbelievable that we have come such a distance in such a short time, to see a young African-American man elected president of the United States."

It's difficult to overstate the significance of the election of President Barack Obama.

As recently as the 1950s, polls showed that the majority of Americans said they would never vote for a black person for president, no matter how qualified. But in 2007, then-Sen. Obama, speaking at a historically black church in Alabama on the 42nd anniversary of the Selma march, talked about our country's great progress in race relations. America, according to Obama, is "90 percent of the way there." Obama said: "I'm here because somebody marched for our freedom. I'm here because y'all sacrificed for me. I stand on the shoulders of giants. I thank the Moses generation. But we have got to remember now that Joshua still had a job to do. ... The previous generation, the Moses generation, pointed the way. They took us 90 percent of the way there. But we (the 'Joshua generation') still got that 10 percent in order to cross over to the other side."

Now this "90 percent" occurred before Obama's election and re-election, so presumably we carved into the remaining 10 percent. But, oh what a difference a few years makes. Two things occurred.

First, the election of a black person did not bring about the expected "hope and change." In fact, the percentage of blacks living in poverty *increased* under Obama. Shortly before Obama's election, a supporter at a campaign rally named Peggy Joseph famously gushed about what an Obama victory would mean: "I wouldn't have to worry about putting gas in my car. I wouldn't have to worry about paying my mortgage. You know — if I help him, he'll help me." Well, guess what. Barbara Bush was right when she said, "Your success as a family, our success as a society, depends not on what happens at the White House but on what happens inside your house."

In 1992, the Department of Justice's Bureau of Justice Statistics examined the 75 most populous counties. Turns out the jury is *less* likely to convict a black defendant of a felony than a white defendant. The study found that "in 12 of the 14 types of crimes (felonies including murder, rape and other serious crimes) for which data was collected, the conviction rate for blacks is lower than that of whites." Similarly, in 2013, the National Institute of Justice, the research and evaluation agency of the DOJ, published their study of whether the police, as a result of racial bias, stop blacks more than other drivers. The conclusion? Any racial disparity in traffic stops is due to "differences in offending" in addition to "differences in exposure to the police" and "differences in driving patterns."

My uncle Eddie, a barber in Chattanooga, Tennessee, immersed himself in local Republican politics. He died 20 years before Obama got elected. He would've been stunned that the country of segregation in which he was born could evolve so that his nephew would see the election of a black president. But he would likely have been even more astonished at how quickly Martin Luther King's dream of a colorblind society has turned into a quest to purge the town square of Confederate statues. He would have been shocked that a group called Black Lives Matter, given credibility by the Obama administration, issued a "list of demands" of white people.

In eight years, we've gone from the election of the first black president to a call for campus "safe spaces" to combat alleged racist "microaggressions." Uncle Eddie would have called this moving the goal post.

'Uncle Tom' Is More Destructive Than the 'N-word'

September 21, 2017

The pejorative "Uncle Tom" causes more damage than does the word "n——."

The "N-word," when used by a white person as an epithet against a black person, is an insult, designed to convey to the recipient that he or she is a second-class citizen. It is designed to make one feel inferior. But it hasn't worked. My parents, as did the parents of my friends, said no one can make you feel inferior without your permission. Lesson learned. For decades, tests measuring self-esteem show that teenage black boys and girls test higher than do white boys and white girls.

"Uncle Tom," on the other hand, when used by a black person as an epithet *against* another black person, is designed to do one thing and one thing only — to label that person as a traitor, a sellout, as a black person who colludes with white racists to undermine the success of black people.

During my pre-election debate at an inner-city black church in Los Angeles against Roland Martin of "NewsOne," a "black" news show on cable channel TV One, Martin advised me to "get in touch with my blackness." My crime? I supported the candidacy of Donald Trump, and predicted he would attract a greater share of the black vote than did Mitt Romney. I suggested that the damage done to the black family by the welfare state was far more than the degree of racism in today's America.

Because of blacker-than-thou people like Martin, the black community is *not* having a robust debate about, for example, whether there is a causal connection between the welfare state and the growing number of fatherless households.

How bad is this lack of critical thinking? During the O.J. Simpson murder trial, a New Jersey high school teacher wrote about the reaction to the case by his mostly black and brown students. Out of 110 students, only four thought Simpson actually did it. Whenever anyone dared suggest an alternative theory, that possibly Simpson himself might have murdered two people, he or she was denounced as a sympathizer for the wrong side. Several thought Kato Kaelin, Simpson's houseguest, did it. Another thought O.J. Simpson's friend Al Cowlings did it, despite a complete and utter lack of evidence. The teacher observed that the black females in his class exerted what he called "social control" over the others in the class to induce unanimity on Simpson's innocence.

Because of the intolerance of different points of view in the black community, we are not having a fact-based debate about the allegation of "systemic" racism in the criminal justice system. The real "traitors" are those who continue to push a false narrative about the alleged "proliferation" of anti-black police brutality, when, according to the Centers for Disease Control, police killings of blacks are down nearly 75 percent since 1968. In Chicago, Mayor Rahm Emanuel admitted that the Black Lives Matter movement has made officers reluctant to proactively police, and that cops have become increasingly passive: "There's no doubt Ferguson, Baltimore, New York, Cleveland, in my view, have put the genie out of the bottle. ... Unless we deal with backing them up, the gang members know (police) are not putting their hands on them because they don't want to be prosecuted, whether it be by public opinion or by the court. ... We have allowed our police department to get fetal, and it is having a direct consequence. ... They have pulled back from the ability to interdict. ... They don't want to be a news story themselves, they don't want their career ended early, and it's having an impact." Crime in many areas of the country has increased, victimizing the very people the Black Lives Matter movement claims to care about.

The real traitors are those who refuse to have a conversation about race-based preferences, even though those admitted to college under affirmative action are far likelier to drop out of college due to a mismatch of skills and school.

The real traitors are those who refuse to look at the obvious connection between the rise of fatherless households in the black community and the welfare state. In 1965, 25 percent of black kids were born outside of wedlock. That figure today is 71 percent. Today 29 percent of white kids are born outside of wedlock. Yet we do not have a serious debate about the causal connection between the welfare state and the No. 1 domestic problem in the country — the rise of fatherless households. But to even raise this issue makes a black person a "traitor" who is "blaming the victim"?

The executive editor of The New York Times, Dean Baquet, a black man, recently acknowledged left-wing intolerance. "The left," he said, "as a rule, does not want to hear thoughtful disagreement." The black left, as a rule, does not believe that there *is* such a thing as thoughtful disagreement.

The National Anthem Protests —
Do Facts Matter?

September 28, 2017

Where was the angry left when Supreme Court Justice Ruth Bader Ginsburg called the national anthem protests "dumb and disrespectful"?

Let's focus on the "dumb" part.

NFL player Colin Kaepernick, who started the protests, did so over the supposed widespread instances of police brutality against blacks. Kaepernick said, "I am not going to stand up to show pride in a flag for a country that oppresses black people and people of color. ... There are bodies in the street and people getting paid leave and getting away with murder." According to the Centers for Disease Control, since 1968 police killings of blacks have *declined* nearly 75 percent. According to The Washington Post, almost 500 whites were killed by cops in 2015, an average of *more* than one a day. Two hundred fifty-nine blacks were killed by the police. Most suspects killed by police had a weapon.

Now for some perspective.

Do you know anyone who has been struck by lightning? Neither do most people. Yet each year an average of about 300 Americans are killed or injured by lightning. That's approximately 40 more than the number of blacks killed by the police in 2015. Is there an "epidemic" of Americans being struck and injured by lightning? We don't know the number of black men injured by lightning every year, but let's assume the number is 7 percent of the total people struck by lightning, mirroring the percentage of the black male population in

America. That brings the average number of black men injured by lightning to about 21.

Out of the 965 people killed by the police in 2015 (as of Dec. 24), the Post reported (on Dec. 26) that "less than 4 percent" involved an unarmed black man and a white cop, the fact pattern most commonly referred to by anti-police activists like Black Lives Matter. Last year, The Washington Post put the number of unarmed black men killed by the police at 17, less than the number of blacks likely struck by lightning. Twenty-two unarmed whites were killed by the police. *Any* death that results from police misconduct is one death too many, but the point is that police killing of a suspect is rare, no matter the race of the suspect or the cop. And a police shooting of an unarmed black male is still more rare.

But blacks are routinely and disproportionately being stopped, pulled over and/or arrested due to police misconduct, right?

No, not according to numerous studies, many by the government. Take traffic stops. In 2013, the National Institute of Justice, the research and evaluation agency of the Department of Justice, published a study of whether the police, as a result of racial bias, stop blacks more than other drivers. The conclusion? Any racial disparity in traffic stops is due to "differences in offending" in addition to "differences in exposure to the police" and "differences in driving patterns."

According to Philippe Lemoine, writing in National Review, a white person is, on average, *more* likely to have interactions with the police in any year than a black person, 20.7 percent vs. 17.5 percent. It is true that a black person is more likely to have multiple contacts with the police. But according to the data, multiple contacts with the police are rare, as well. Lemoine writes that 1.2 percent of white men have more than three contacts with the police in a year versus 1.5 percent of black men.

But what about the experience of a black person with the police versus that of a white person? The DOJ's Bureau of Justice Statistics regularly studies this, too. Every year, the BJS surveys a representative sample of 70,000 people. Among the questions, the survey asks whether respondents had contact with the police in the last 12 months. If the answer is "yes," the survey asks a number of follow-up questions, including about use of force.

Let's concentrate on cases involving use of force.

Lemoine writes: "Only 0.6 percent of black men experience physical force by the police in any given year, while approximately 0.2 percent of white men do. ... Moreover, keep in mind that these tallies of police violence include violence that is legally justified." And keep in mind the much higher levels of crime by mostly black males. It is estimated that half of all homicides are committed by, and mostly against, black males.

In 1995, the federal government looked at 42,500 defendants in the nation's 75 largest counties. A government statistician, Patrick A. Langan, found "no evidence that, in the places where blacks in the United States have most of their contacts with the justice system, that system treats them more harshly than whites." So much for the so-called "institutional racism" in the criminal justice system.

Recently, in Illinois, in a kids' 8-and-under football league, the entire team, which appeared to be all black, *including the coach,* took a knee during the national anthem. Asked why, one third-grade player parroted Kaepernick, saying, according to the coach, "Because black people are getting killed, and nobody's going to jail."

Trump Not Letting Media Turn Puerto Rico Into His 'Katrina'

October 5, 2017

President Donald Trump punched back hard against the mayor of San Juan, Puerto Rico, who accused him of insufficient concern about her island. In doing so, Trump shows that he learned from President George W. Bush's mistakes. Bush 43 seemed to expect a certain level of fairness and civility from the media.

When, for example, Sen. Ted Kennedy, about the prewar Iraq intelligence, said, "Before the war, week after week after week after week, we were told lie after lie after lie after lie," the Bush White House did not aggressively push back against that venomous assertion. When critics made the hideous accusations that President George W. Bush was "lying us into war," the White House did little to fight back. That, at least, is the assessment of both former Vice President Dick Cheney and former Secretary of Defense Don Rumsfeld, whom I had the privilege of interviewing. Cheney and Rumsfeld lamented their failure to aggressively and loudly refute the accusation. Why didn't they fight back? Both told me that they considered the charges so incredibly offensive and easily refuted that few would believe it.

President Trump makes no such assumptions. One readily imagines a President Trump reaching for his Twitter account to aggressively counter such a hideous accusation.

But the "Bush lied, people died" mantra would stick, at least for Democrats. Many Democrats believe George W. Bush either lied about the intel on Iraq's weapons of mass destruction or that there is a possibility that he lied. The claim remains a stain on the Republican brand, a party that, to many on the left, took its country into a war that cost thousands of lives over an intentional lie.

Never mind the conclusion of the Commission on the Intelligence Capabilities of the United States Regarding Weapons of Mass Destruction, which investigated whether the Bush administration intentionally misled the nation. It concluded: "The Intelligence Community's performance in assessing Iraq's pre-war weapons of mass destruction programs was a major intelligence failure. The failure was not merely that the Intelligence Community's assessments were wrong. There were also serious shortcomings in the way these assessments were made and communicated to policymakers." In a letter to President Bush, the commission said, "After a thorough review, the Commission found no indication that the Intelligence Community distorted the evidence regarding Iraq's weapons of mass destruction. What the intelligence professionals told you about Saddam Hussein's programs was what they believed. They were simply wrong."

A President Trump would have blasted social media for "ignoring" the commission's findings — and rained insults upon insults on "reporters" like then-Associated Press Washington bureau chief Ron Fournier who, despite the commission's conclusion, publicly stated that Bush lied us into war in Iraq. Trump would have blistered him.

Trump, in the case of Puerto Rico and Hurricane Maria, refuses to let media and politicians like Rep. Luis Gutierrez, D-Ill., who called the federal response in Puerto Rico "disgraceful," turn this into Trump's Katrina. After Katrina, President Bush got blamed for the shortcomings and political infighting between local and state authorities. Recall how rapper Kanye West, during a fundraiser for Katrina victims, claimed, "George Bush doesn't care about black people." Then-senatorial candidate Claire McCaskill even said, "George Bush let people die on rooftops in New Orleans because they were poor and because they were black."

As for Hurricane Maria and Trump's response, San Juan Mayor Carmen Yulin Cruz said: "We are dying here. ... And you are killing us with the inefficiency and the bureaucracy. We will make it with or without you. ... I am done being polite. I am done being politically correct. I am mad as hell, because my people's lives are at stake."

Trump, in a series of tweets, fired back:

"The Mayor of San Juan, who was very complimentary only a few days ago, has now been told by the Democrats that you must be nasty to Trump.

"...Such poor leadership ability by the Mayor of San Juan, and others in Puerto Rico, who are not able to get their workers to help. They...

"...want everything to be done for them when it should be a community effort. 10,000 Federal workers now on Island doing a fantastic job.

"The military and first responders, despite no electric, roads, phones etc., have done an amazing job. Puerto Rico was totally destroyed."

`The facts do suggest that the damage inflicted by Maria overwhelmed the island's already poor infrastructure making it nearly impossible to deliver supplies local authorities. Trump, unlike Bush, refused to be labeled as the president who "doesn't care."

Bravo, Mr. President. Bravo.

If 'No One Wants to Take Our Guns,'
Stop Saying the Opposite

October 12, 2017

Almost immediately after the Las Vegas shooting came the calls for "common sense" gun control. The quest almost always begins with a reassurance that "no one wants to take away your guns."

Not everyone read the memo.

Nelson Shields, founder of Handgun Control, Inc., the organization that became the Brady Campaign to Prevent Gun Violence, in a 1976 interview could not have been more clear about his group's goals: "Our ultimate goal — total control of handguns in the United States — is going to take time. My estimate is from seven to 10 years. The first problem is to slow down the increasing number of handguns being produced and sold in this country. The second problem is to get handguns registered. And the final problem is to make the possession of all handguns and all handgun ammunition — except for the military, policemen, licensed security guards, licensed sporting clubs, and licensed gun collectors — totally illegal."

In 1993, a Los Angeles Times editorial called for the repeal of the Second Amendment: "You will not feel safe, your children will not be safe, until there are almost no guns on the streets and in homes. No guns, period, except for those held by law enforcement officers and a few others, including qualified hunters and collectors. ... We must, as a nation, move toward a very different model, one that presumptively bars private citizens from owning a firearm unless they can demonstrate a special need and ability to do so. ... We think the time has come for Americans to tell the truth about guns. They are not for us; we cannot handle them. They kill people, our children included. It's time to get rid of them. Period."

Fast-forward to the Las Vegas shooting. The Washington Post columnist Eugene Robinson calls for a gun "buyback": "A real gun debate has to look at that fact: 300 million guns. And we need, you know, to look at what was done in a place like Australia, where they had a gun buyback. And gun control is permissible, according to the Supreme Court. And so if Congress were to decide — it won't happen — were to decide that automatic assault rifles, long guns ... (and) military-style weapons are something that citizens should not have, they should be police and military only, and we're going to buy them back, that would have an impact. ... And that's what the debate ought to be."

Recall that Hillary Clinton, during the 2016 election, also gushed over the allegedly successful Australian gun buyback program: "Australia had a huge mass killing about 20, 25 years ago. Canada did as well, so did the UK. In reaction, they passed much stricter gun laws. ... The Australian government as part of trying to clamp down on the availability of automatic weapons, offered a good price for buying hundreds of thousands of guns and basically clamped down going forward, in terms of having more of a background check approach — more of a permitting approach."

True, Australia, over 20 years ago, banned semi-automatic and self-loading rifles, as well as self-loading and pump-action shotguns. The government offered up to a one-year grace period during which it would buy back the banned firearms at preset "market value" prices, financed by a tax on health insurance. After that, people possessing the banned weapons would be subject to strict penalties, including imprisonment.

But did Australia's gun buyback program reduce violent gun crime?

No, according to John Lott of the Crime Prevention Research Center. "Their firearms homicide rate," said Lott, "had been falling for a decade prior to the buyback. It continued falling at the same rate after the buyback. There was no sudden drop, just a fairly constant decline that continued even as gun ownership rose back up to previous levels. The armed robbery rate rose in the first five years after the buyback. After another 10 years, the rate had fallen to pre-buyback levels."

The near-term "common sense" goal of the gun controllers is to ban the "bump stock" that enabled the shooter to turn a semi-automatic into a fully automatic weapon. Never mind that of the modern mass shootings in America, only one killer used a machine gun: Stephen Paddock. And where was this "common sense" when President Barack Obama's ATF approved the bump stock, pronouncing it a part, not a weapon? California has some of the most stringent gun laws in the country, yet has experienced mass shootings, including the San Bernardino shooting in 2015, where 14 were killed.

This is not to say that nothing can be done to make a Las Vegas-style shooting more difficult. But most of these things will be done by private actors. Las Vegas hotel/casino owner Steve Wynn, for example, said his Vegas resorts already had additional security measures in place.

The "common sense" goal of many "gun control activists" is not a ban on this or that feature but a ban on civilian ownership of guns. Just ask the Los Angeles Times.

Yes, Weinstein Accusers Are Brave — So Were Jones, Willey and Broaddrick

October 19, 2017

In the wake of the Harvey Weinstein scandal, former Secretary of State Hillary Clinton, among others, praised the Weinstein accusers for their "courage." For decades, Weinstein, a big Democratic donor who could make or break Hollywood careers, apparently preyed on young women. Over 30 women have now come forth, with five alleging rape.

But where were Hollywood's social justice warriors the last 30 years?

After all, Hollywood insiders call Weinstein's behavior Hollywood's worst kept secret. The television series "Entourage," based on the world of Hollywood agents, portrayed an obnoxious, browbeating character, Harvey Weingard, clearly based on Weinstein. On NBC's series "30 Rock," one character made the following joke: "I turned down intercourse with Harvey Weinstein on no less than three occasions — out of five."

At the 2013 Oscar awards show, host Seth MacFarlane, after reading the names of the five nominees in the supporting actress category, joked, "Congratulations. You five ladies no longer have to pretend to be attracted to Harvey Weinstein." Today MacFarlane says, "I couldn't resist the opportunity to take a hard swing in his direction," after his friend, actress Jessica Barth, confided that she had been sexually harassed by Weinstein in his hotel room in 2011.

So, many in the Hollywood industry said and did nothing — until now. The courageous women coming forward deserve praise and encouragement for speaking out. But where was this support for the accusers of Bill and Hillary Clinton?

Former Arkansas staffer Paula Jones accused then-Gov. and presidential candidate Bill Clinton of sexual harassment. Clinton aide James Carville famously said, "If you drag a hundred-dollar bill through a trailer park, you never know what you'll find." Jones said she sought help from the National Organization for Women, but they refused to support her.

Kathleen Willey, on "60 Minutes," described being a victim of alleged sexual battery by Clinton in the Oval Office. Willey, a Clinton campaign volunteer, says that Clinton took her hand and placed it on his aroused genitalia: "He touched my breasts with his hand ... and then he whispered ... 'I've wanted to do this ever since I laid eyes on you.' ... He took my hand, and he put it ... on his genitals." Willey said she managed to push him away. Not only did the left's social justice warriors refuse to support her feminist Gloria Steinem actually defended Clinton! Days after Willey's appearance, Steinem wrote, "Even if (Willey's) allegations are true, the President is not guilty of sexual harassment. ... (Willey) pushed him away, she said, and it never happened again. In other words, President Clinton took 'no' for an answer." Incredible.

Juanita Broaddrick, on "Dateline NBC," accused Clinton of raping her when he was Arkansas attorney general and a gubernatorial candidate: "I first pushed him away. I just told him 'no.' ... He tries to kiss me again. He starts biting on my lip. ... And then he forced me down on the bed. I just was very frightened. I tried to get away from him. I told him 'no.' ... He wouldn't listen to me."

Broaddrick also claims that two weeks after the alleged rape, Hillary Clinton verbally intimidated her. According to Broaddrick, Hillary approached her at a political event: "She came over to me, took ahold of my hand and said, 'I've heard so much about you and I've been dying to meet you. ... I just want you to know how much that Bill and I appreciate what you do for him.' ... (Hillary Clinton) took ahold of my hand and squeezed it and said, 'Do you understand? Everything that you do.' I could have passed out at that moment, and I got my hand from hers and I left. ... She was just holding onto my hand. Because I had started to turn away from her and she held onto my hand and she said, 'Do you understand?

Everything that you do,' I mean, cold chills went up my spine. That's the first time I became afraid of that woman."

What was the media's response to Broaddrick's accusation?

It appears that the *only* national reporter to ever ask Bill Clinton about Broaddrick's allegations was Sam Donaldson. After Donaldson's question, Clinton said, "I have decided ... that I would allow all future questions to be answered by my attorneys." Donaldson quickly tried again, asking the then-President to "simply deny it." Clinton responded, "There's been a statement made by my attorney. He speaks for me, and I think he spoke quite clearly." And that was that.

Where were the Hollywood social justice warriors back then, when the accused was Bill Clinton? After all, Hillary Clinton once said that when women make allegations of abuse, "everyone should be believed at first until they are disbelieved based on evidence." Didn't Madeleine Albright, the first female secretary of state, repeatedly say, "There's a special place in hell for women who don't help each other!"?

Based on the way the left treated Jones, Willey, Broaddrick and other Bill and Hillary Clinton accusers, that "special place" could get rather crowded.

My Own Harvey Weinstein Experience

October 26, 2017

I knew of Harvey Weinstein, and I'd heard that he possessed the power to make or break careers, that he was bombastic and that he pushed people around. But that pretty much was the extent of it. After all, this is Hollywood, where only a small percent of would-be actors and actresses in the Screen Actors Guild earn enough to make a full-time living in their chosen profession. In this town — and especially in the acting community — anxiety is the norm.

A friend and former studio executive once invited me to a cocktail party he was hosting to celebrate some recent milestone of his entertainment-industry company. It was, at least at first, a quiet wine and cheese kind of affair.

Enter Harvey Weinstein.

My friend introduced me to him. Before I could respond, Weinstein said, "I know who you are. You're the guy who supports the war in Iraq. You know Bush lied us into it!" I decided to just ignore it. What an a—hole, I thought to myself. But Weinstein wasn't about to let it go. He repeated the accusation that Bush "lied" us into the war. Again, I acted as if I didn't hear it, until, that is, he said it again.

OK, it's on.

"A lie means an intent to deceive. OK, Harvey, how did he lie, Harvey?" I said loudly.

"Everyone knows he lied," he said.

"If everybody knows it," I said, "it should be easy for you to come up with a lie. Give me a lie, Harvey. One!"

He muttered something about "bad intel."

"Bad intel and lies are two different things, Harvey. You said 'lie.' Give me the lie!"

At this point, Weinstein turned and walked away. My friend, who had known Weinstein for years, said, "I've never seen anyone speak to Harvey that way." To which I said, "What's he going to do to me? Not put me in his next movie?"

Since that little party, Weinstein has been outed as a serial predator over a period of 30 years, with more than 50 women making accusations. According to The New York Times, "Mr. Weinstein has reached at least eight settlements with women, according to two company officials speaking on the condition of anonymity."

Successful screenwriter Scott Rosenberg, who credits the Weinstein brothers at Miramax for giving him his start, now shamefully admits, "Everybody knew."

In a recent Facebook post, Rosenberg writes: "Let's be perfectly clear about one thing: Everybody (expletive) knew. Not that he was raping. No, that we never heard. But we were aware of a certain pattern of overly-aggressive behavior that was rather dreadful. We knew about the man's hunger; his fervor; his appetite. There was nothing secret about this voracious rapacity; like a gluttonous ogre out of the Brothers Grimm. All couched in vague promises of potential movie roles. ...

"And to me, if Harvey's behavior is the most reprehensible thing one can imagine, a not-so-distant second is the current flood of sanctimonious denial and condemnation that now crashes upon these shores of rectitude in gloppy tides of (expletive) righteousness. Because everybody (expletive) knew. And do you know how I am sure this is true? Because I was there. And I saw you. And I talked about it with you. You, the big producers; you, the big directors; you, the big agents; you, the big financiers. And you, the big rival studio chiefs; you, the big actors; you, the big actresses; you, the big models. You, the big journalists; you, the big screenwriters; you, the big rock stars; you, the big restaurateurs; you, the big politicians."

Incredibly, Weinstein's contract actually acknowledges his abusive behavior, and seemingly expected it to continue. The entertainment news website TMZ writes that Harvey Weinstein's

2015 employment contract with The Weinstein Company calls for him to reimburse the company: "If he gets sued for sexual harassment or any other 'misconduct' that results in a settlement or judgment against TWC, all Weinstein has to do is pay what the company's out, along with a fine, and he's in the clear."

His contract required him to pay fines, writes TMZ, "'of $250,000 for the first such instance, $500,000 for the second such instance, $750,000 for the third such instance, and $1,000,000 for each additional instance.'

"The contract says as long as Weinstein pays, it constitutes a 'cure' for the misconduct and no further action can be taken. Translation — Weinstein could be sued over and over and as long as he wrote a check, he keeps his job."

The Weinstein revelations have sparked a number of accusations against other prominent Hollywood figures — and it might just be the tip of the iceberg.

Oh, and, sure enough, after my testy exchange with Weinstein at the cocktail party, when his next movie came out, I wasn't in it.

Our Ex-Presidents' Insincere Praise of 'American Generosity'

November 2, 2017

All five living former Presidents recently came together at a benefit concert for victims of this year's devastating hurricanes. A month earlier, they broadcast an appeal for Americans to donate for hurricane relief efforts.

Former President Jimmy Carter praised the generosity of Americans: "Across this great country, Americans have answered the call." So did former President George W. Bush, who said, "That special calling that compels us when others are down to step up and do whatever it takes." Former President Barack Obama said: "We could not be prouder of the response of Americans. When they see their neighbors, when they see their friends, when they see strangers in need, Americans step up." Former President Bill Clinton said, "We've been volunteering since before the Constitution, when Benjamin Franklin organized the first volunteer fire department in Philadelphia."

But the former Presidents' records of expanding government belie their rhetoric about the generosity of Americans.

In the case of President Carter, in 1978, he created FEMA, the Federal Emergency Management Agency, displacing, in some cases, much of the local, state and private sector assistance that the distressed once relied on. But after Carter established FEMA, something interesting occurred. The country experienced an uptick in declared natural disasters, which triggered an influx of federal money. FEMA was intended to handle civil defense and public evacuations and to ensure continuity of government in the event of nuclear or other attacks. But after FEMA was determined to have mishandled the response to Hurricane Hugo in 1988, the Loma Prieta earthquake in San Francisco in 1989 and Hurricane Andrew in 1992, President Clinton reorganized it, elevating the organization to Cabinet status. It is no surprise that states and localities started relying on the Feds more and spending less on things like snow-removal equipment, freeing the money for other projects.

Carter also signed the Community Reinvestment Act to encourage banks to lend to "underrepresented minority" loan applicants. President Clinton put teeth into the law, which, among other factors, had the effect of altering lending standards for the entire industry. If Presidents Carter and Clinton believed in American generosity, why force lenders to do that which their basic kindness would have them do anyway?

In the case of President George Herbert Walker Bush, he signed the Americans with Disabilities Act. Despite its noble name and intentions, the ADA actually made it *more* difficult for a job applicant with a disability to find employment. "Since the highly touted Americans with Disabilities Act passed ... a decade ago," reported the Los Angeles Times in 1999, "supposedly offering new protections for the disabled, things have worsened significantly. ... During the Clinton administration, unemployment of working-age people with disabilities has soared from a horrendous 66 percent to a disastrous 75 percent. For those with severe disabilities, for example those who cannot walk, the unemployment rate, once 87 percent, is rising."

What explained the uptick in unemployment? Though ADA supporters claimed the act provided incentives for both employer and prospective disabled employee, the law of unintended consequences kicked in. Employers worried, "Will I face a lawsuit should I need to fire a disabled person? How much must I spend in order to 'accommodate' a disabled employee?" If President Bush 41 truly believed the things he says about American generosity, and his rhetoric and about our nation's "thousand points of light," why force an employer to be charitable?

President George W. Bush, to deal with the carnage caused by the government intrusion into the housing market, bailed out banks and other institutions with TARP, the Troubled Asset Relief Program. So we experienced even more government intrusion into the housing market in response to the damage caused by forcing lenders to, in essence, practice generosity.

Former President Obama, of course, signed into law Obamacare, in large part because the left feels health care is a right and that private insurance should be forced to sign those with pre-existing illnesses. So much for the charity of Americans to deal with those who cannot otherwise afford health care or health care insurance.

Now Clinton deserves credit for signing the welfare reform act of 1996, which for the first time put caps on welfare along with time limits. Able-bodied and able-minded people got off the couch and into the job market. But for the most part, these Presidents, while in office, expanded the federal government to do things that could and should be done by the very same American people they insist are so compassionate.

Black-on-Black Racism at Cornell

November 9, 2017

A Rasmussen poll taken in 2013 asked American adults, "Are most white Americans racist?" "Are most Hispanic Americans racist?" and "Are most black Americans racist?" Of the three groups, the winner was blacks.

Thirty-seven percent said most blacks were racist; 18 percent felt most Hispanics were racist; and 15 percent said most whites were racist.

Thirty-eight percent of whites felt most blacks were racist. Even blacks agreed, with 31 percent saying most blacks were racist, while 24 percent of blacks thought most whites racist and 15 percent believed most Hispanics were racist.

This brings us to the Cornell University's Black Students United and whether the organization is engaging in racism — against *blacks*. The BSU complains that the prestigious Ivy League school admits too many blacks — from Africa and the Caribbean. "We demand that Cornell Admissions to come up with a plan to actively increase the presence of underrepresented Black students on this campus," the BSU student group said in its demands. "We define underrepresented Black students as Black Americans who have several generations (more than two) in this country."

Hold the phone. Isn't the mantra of modern higher education "diversity," "inclusion" and "overcoming disadvantage"? If so, the black African and Caribbean students would seem to nail all three.

Maybe the problem is that it is tough to explain why so many black foreign applicants outperform America-born blacks on what some call "culturally biased" standardized tests. A 2007 study by Princeton and University of Pennsylvania sociologists examined the standardized test scores of black students enrolled at 28 selective universities. As to the SAT, the test most colleges use as an important factor in offering admission, the study found that foreign-born black college-bound students earned a statistically significant advantage on SAT scores, averaging a score of 1250 (out of 1600) compared to 1193 average points for their American black counterparts. This explains, in large part, why first- or second-generation black immigrants made up 27 percent of the black student bodies at colleges nationwide. In the Ivy League, black immigrants comprised 41 percent of black students.

What is the basis for the black students' protest? Don't black foreigners face even more obstacles? After all, America spends more on education, K through 12, than the top 34 industrialized countries save Switzerland, Austria, Norway and Luxembourg. New York City and Washington, D.C., annually spend approximately $21,000 and $15,000 per student, respectively.

BSU might want to consider the letter to the editor of The Wall Street Journal written by a man from Congo:

"I grew up in the Congo and have numerous friends in the U.S. from the Congo and other African countries who are here for an education or a better life. Every one of them is grateful for the opportunity to secure an excellent education. ... Most come here from different cultures with minimal money and limited English language skills. Interestingly, I've never heard one complain about discrimination, obstacles or being a victim. Rather, they are grateful. Juxtapose this with Cornell's Black Students United (BSU) whose members feel they should be treated better than every other color or race if they have ancestors who've been here for more than two generations.

"The counterintuitive posturing of American blacks denying other blacks from Africa or the Caribbean is appalling. First-generation African or Caribbean students have more obstacles to overcome to get into any university, much less a prestigious one like Cornell. Furthermore, the liberal American blacks who worship at the altar of 'diversity' and 'victimhood' should welcome real Africans or Caribbeans versus seeking preferences for those

American blacks who truly have the superior advantage of having grown up in the U.S.

"If my Congolese friends are grateful for their opportunities here and have more challenges to overcome, why should American blacks get special treatment? Call this action what it is: racism. And it's being pushed and protected under the guise of alleged victimization and preferential treatment at the expense of others of all colors and walks of life. So I challenge the BSU folks to start focusing on the concept of succeeding in life instead of always dwelling on the idea that the system is rigged against them."

The black immigrant culture rejects the victicrat mentality embraced by so many American blacks. In "The Triple Package," a 2014 book about immigrants' children, a son of Nigerian-born parents says, "If you start thinking about or becoming absorbed in the mentality that the whole system is against us, then you cannot succeed."

Rather than complain about the success of foreign-born blacks, why not give failing urban schools some competition through vouchers to give parents greater choice in where to educate their children, a policy currently pushed by the Trump administration? In the Detroit public school district, for example, just 7 percent of eighth-graders are proficient or better in reading and just 4 percent are sufficient or better in math, despite total expenditures per student of over $18,000, according to the 2015 National Assessment of Educational Progress tests.

Isn't *this* the real problem?

No, Colin Kaepernick Is No
Muhammad Ali

November 16, 2017

GQ magazine named former NFL quarterback Colin Kaepernick its 2017 "Citizen of the Year." In doing so, GQ overlooked NFL Houston Texans' J.J. Watt, who raised some $37 million for hurricane relief. Many of Kaepernick's supporters liken his protest to that of boxer Muhammad Ali, who refused to be inducted into the military. The comparison is not well-taken.

For whatever reason, Kaepernick chose not to give the magazine an interview, passing up an opportunity to clearly explain the purpose of his protest. At first, Kaepernick insisted his protest was about the alleged epidemic of police brutality against blacks. Shortly after he started his protest, Kaepernick said: "There's a lot of things that need to change. One specifically is police brutality. There's people being murdered unjustly and not being held accountable. The cops are getting paid leave for killing people. That's not right."

Contrast this with Muhammad Ali's protest. He argued that his religious beliefs made him a conscientious objector who ought not be forced to join the military. In doing so, Ali faced up to five years in prison and was stripped of his ability to fight in the U.S. for more than three years, his prime years as an athlete. While the heavyweight title-holder avoided prison during his appeals process — that ended up in the Supreme Court — he was forced to hand over his passport, which prevented him from fighting overseas, as well.

Banned from boxing and stripped of his world heavyweight title, Ali argued his case on the road, speaking at a number of colleges and universities, where he repeatedly stated that he would rather abide by his religious convictions rather than violate them in order to make money. Martin Luther King Jr. urged his followers to "admire (Ali's) courage. He is giving up fame. He is giving up millions of dollars to do what his conscience tells him is right."

By contrast, Kaepernick wants to have it both ways. The NFL allows players to stand or not, depending upon their own choice. So the league actually gives players permission to stand or not to stand for the national anthem. In Ali's case, his refusal to join the military cost him the ability to earn a living in his chosen profession.

The Supreme Court eventually sided unanimously with Ali, ruling that the appeal board failed to properly specify the reason why Ali's application for a conscientious-objector exemption had been denied. The ruling required Ali's conviction to be overturned, and the court said the record shows that Ali's "beliefs are founded on tenets of the Muslim religion as he understands them." After his Supreme Court victory, Ali could have sued for lost wages, arguing that he was illegally forbidden from working as a fighter. Ali refused, arguing that he would rather look ahead then exact revenge.

Kaepernick, on the other hand, filed a grievance against the NFL, claiming the owners "colluded" against hiring this mediocre-quarterback-turned-locker-room-distraction.

What about the merits of Kaepernick's argument? Is there an epidemic of police brutality against blacks? The answer is no.

According to the Centers for Disease Control, police shootings against blacks have declined almost 75 percent since 1968. Of the 963 people shot and killed by police in 2016, 233 were black, and 466 were white. Most people could not name a white person killed by the police, because the media are far less interested in a white person killed by a cop than a black person killed by one. Last year, a grand total of 17 unarmed blacks were killed by the police, according to The Washington Post. Contrast this with the approximately 6,000 to 7,000 blacks killed annually, almost all — as many as 90 percent — by other blacks. Where is Kaepernick on the fact that the No. 1 cause of preventable death for young blacks is homicide, while the No. 1 cause of preventable death for young white men is "unintentional injuries," or accidents?

San Antonio Spurs coach Gregg Popovich, who supports Kaepernick, said: "It's easier for white people because we haven't lived that experience. It's difficult for many white people to understand the day-to-day feeling that many black people have to deal with. ...

"When somebody like Kaepernick brings attention to this, and others who have, it makes people have to face the issue because it's too easy to let it go because it's not their daily experience. If it's not your daily experience, you don't understand it."

As to Popovich's assertion about the "day-to-day feeling that many black people have to deal with," what of the 1997 Time/CNN poll that found 89 percent of black teens found little or no racism in their day-to-day lives? And more black teens than white teens agreed that "failure to take advantage of available opportunities" was a bigger problem than racism. And this was 20 years ago, before the election and re-election of a black President.

Kaepernick's protest was bogus from the start, and it only helped to create greater unnecessary tension between the black community and the police. "Citizen of the Year," indeed.

I Got Fired for Calling Out Liberal Hypocrisy on Clinton Accusers

November 23, 2017

It was bizarre watching KABC TalkRadio in Los Angeles — my hypocritical ex-employer — hold a televised press conference. It turns out that one of the station's news anchors, Leeann Tweeden, claims Sen. Al Franken groped her. In 2006, Tweeden said, before Franken became a senator, he and she participated in a USO tour to entertain the troops in the Middle East.

But, claims Tweeden: "(Franken) repeated that actors really need to rehearse everything and that we *must* practice the kiss. I said 'OK' so he would stop badgering me. We did the line leading up to the kiss and then he came at me, put his hand on the back of my head, mashed his lips against mine and aggressively stuck his tongue in my mouth.

"I immediately pushed him away with both of my hands against his chest and told him if he ever did that to me again I wouldn't be so nice about it the next time.

"I walked away. All I could think about was getting to a bathroom as fast as possible to rinse the taste of him out of my mouth.

"I felt disgusted and violated."

Why was the KABC press conference about Franken's misconduct bizarre?

Only a few years earlier, the same KABC radio executive who arranged the Tweeden press conference fired me for calling out the blatant left-wing hypocrisy over allegations not just of groping but of rape. I dared insist that the allegations made against President Bill Clinton by Juanita Broaddrick — who claims that she was raped by Bill Clinton and that then, two weeks after the rape, Hillary Clinton verbally intimidated the alleged rape survivor — should have been taken seriously. "No one cares about this issue," said the very same KABC exec now allegedly incensed over the groping allegation against Franken. As for Broaddrick, the executive screamed, she is "old news," as, he insisted, were Bill and Hillary's treatment of multiple accusers. He burst into my radio studio, with the show in progress, and literally yelled at me for pounding an "irrelevant" topic. Shortly before I got fired, the executive sent this letter to my agent:

"I point out that from 3:15 pm to almost 4 o'clock, Larry is AGAIN talking about Kathleen Willey, Juanita Broderrick (sic), Monica Lewinsky, Paula Jones and somehow linking Hillary Clinton and James Carville to Bill Clinton being a rapist and sexual harasser. This line of discussion is repeated and repeated, day after day. It is neither timely or relevant to today — though I assume Larry thinks it is in some way. It is my opinion that the sheer volume of instances — sometimes multiple times a day — where he brings this old, arcane topic up is very detrimental to the ratings. While there are literally scores of current, important and compelling stories, Larry is talking, again, about an issue from over 20 years ago. For the better part of an hour. Please let me know if you have some idea of how to get it to cease, short of embargoing mentions of the names above. ... It was my understanding that Larry was going to stop by and see me. He has not."

It isn't enough to criticize Bill and Hillary Clinton — so-called advocates for women — for their hypocrisy. What about ABC News' "chief anchor," George Stephanopoulos, who helped set up the "war room" to respond to allegations made by women against Clinton? Stephanopoulos, then a top aide to presidential candidate Bill Clinton, even said, "Bill Clinton has no character problem." How does a partisan like Stephanopoulos, who consistently defended Clinton's behavior and blamed the "Republican attack machine," become the "chief news anchor" of anything, let alone of ABC News? If, at last, much of the country is reassessing their opinion of Bill and Hillary Clinton, what about enablers like Stephanopoulos?

What about media executives, like the one I once worked for, who downplayed the hypocrisy and, in his case, actively attempted to squash any discussion of it? What about these media enablers? Comedian Chelsea Handler recently tweeted: "Imagine being molested by an older man. Then that man denies ever doing it and then goes on and gets elected to United States Senate. What kind of message does that send to young girls everywhere? And men to all the men who abuse women?"

Juanita Broaddrick tweeted back: "I can imagine. I was raped by the Arkansas AG who then becomes Governor & President and NBC held my interview explaining the rape until after his impeachment hearing. But I'm sure you don't want to go there." Handler apologized: "You are right and I apologize to you for not knowing your story. Democrats along with Republicans and the rest of the world's political parties all need to do better and respect the firsthand accounts of victims. I believe you."

Why did Handler not know her story? Blame media decision-makers who ignored or downplayed this issue — and even threatened the careers of those who dared call out the hypocrisy.

Dump Roy Moore

November 30, 2017

It is a political, tactical and moral mistake for Republicans to continue backing Judge Roy Moore for Alabama's Senate seat.

In brief, he has been accused by multiple women of, decades ago, making unwanted and inappropriate sexual advances toward them when they were teenage girls — one as young as 14 — and he was in his 30s. At least four women say he initiated sexual contact with them.

When asked if he thought the Moore allegations were true, Senate Majority Leader Mitch McConnell, R-Ky., said, "I believe the women, yes. ... I think he should step aside" — a sentiment shared, publicly and privately, by nearly all Republican senators.

President Donald Trump at first struck the right chord. After his handpicked Republican candidate lost the primary election, Trump called Moore to congratulate him. Everything was fine, until the allegations. Then Trump said, "If the allegations are true, he should drop out." When the Republican National Committee withdrew its funding for Moore, Trump went along with it.

Then Trump began to twist, and he now says that Moore is innocent until proven guilty, that these are all old claims and that we can't have a lefty in the Senate:

"(Moore) denies it," the President said last week. "Look, he denies it. I mean, if you look at what is really going on, and you look at all the things that have happened over the last 48 hours, he totally denies it. He says it didn't happen. And, you know, you have to listen to him also. You're talking about, he said 40 years ago this did not happen."

Trump then blasted Moore's Democratic opponent, Doug Jones, via Twitter: "The last thing we need in Alabama and the U.S. Senate is a Schumer/Pelosi puppet who is WEAK on Crime, WEAK on the Border, Bad for our Military and our great Vets, Bad for our 2nd Amendment, AND WANTS TO RAISES TAXES TO THE SKY. Jones would be a disaster!"

These are not good enough reasons.

Again, Moore was not Trump's guy. Luther Strange — the incumbent appointed to complete the term of former Sen. Jeff Sessions, who became Attorney General — was Trump's choice. But Steve Bannon, Trump's former aide, wanted Moore, presumably because the former judge supported Bannon's desire to ditch Senate leader Mitch McConnell. Yet during the Luther Strange and Roy Moore debates, the candidates fell all over themselves to argue who would be more closely linked to the Trump agenda. So, no matter who won, he figured to be an ally to the President.

Defenders of Moore ask, why now? After decades in public service, why are these allegations only now coming out? A better question, why the allegations in the first place? Are they credible? But to answer the timing question, the more likely "culprit" is not Democratic opposition, but Harvey Weinstein, whose sexual abuse and misconduct opened the door for other accusers in other fields to come forward. That these allegations are only now being taken seriously is too little too late, but the timing could not have been worse for Moore.

Of course he is "innocent until proven guilty." This is not a court of law. This is politics. Are the defenders of Moore willing to discount all of his accusers but believe the accusers against Bill Clinton?

The voluminous allegations against Harvey Weinstein, a friend and patron of the political left, have forced the Democrats to reconsider their adoration for the likes of Bill Clinton and Ted Kennedy, whose resumes include credible allegations of sexual assault, allegations long ignored.

For now, Republicans occupy the high moral ground, as Democrats, already dealing with allegations of sexual misconduct by

Sen. Al Franken, D-Minn., and Rep. John Conyers, D-Mich., squirm to explain how and why they ignored, downplayed or accepted the sexual behavior of party icons Clinton and Ted Kennedy.

With Moore defenders, in part, circling the wagons on Moore, many Trump voters apparently cannot answer this question: Why did you "overlook" the allegations made by some dozen women against now-President Donald Trump?

That's easy.

Trump was not running against Mother Teresa. Trump ran against Hillary Clinton, a woman against whom a credible allegation was made that she verbally intimidated Juanita Broaddrick just two weeks after Bill Clinton allegedly raped her. Conservative Barbara Olson's book "Hell to Pay" and liberal Christopher Hitchens' book "No One Left to Lie To" depict Hillary as the Toscanini of the "nuts or sluts" strategy effectively employed to malign and marginalize her husband's accusers.

This is the person against whom Donald Trump ran. So, no, Republicans need not apologize for supporting Trump against a person whose actions enabled, covered up for and therefore perpetuated her husband's misconduct.

By supporting Roy Moore, Republicans, on the issue of sexual misconduct, risk turning into the my-guy-wrong-or-wrong hypocrites from across the aisle.

Leadership Malpractice: John Conyers' Resignation Is 50 Years Too Late

December 7, 2017

Rep. John Conyers, D-Mich., hospitalized for an undefined stress-related illness, announced his retirement after serving more than 50 years in the House. Two other Conyers — a son and a great-nephew — immediately announced plans to vie for the elder Conyers' seat. The great-nephew said, "His doctor advised him that the rigor of another campaign would be too much for him just in terms of his health."

Despite his sudden retirement, Conyers "vehemently" denies all accusations that he ever committed sexual harassment. "My legacy can't be compromised or diminished in any way by what we are going through now," Conyers said in a radio interview from the hospital. "This too shall pass. My legacy will continue through my children."

One former aide describes how the congressman, who was driving while she was in the passenger seat, attempted to fondle her: "He was trying to feel me up with his right hand. I kept pushing his hand away. Then he put his hand on my neck and started trying to tickle me. We were on I-75, and he was driving erratically. I was saved by the bell because we got pulled over by the police for the way he was driving." Another former staffer claimed that Conyers would sit "close to (her) while stroking and rubbing (her) thighs," and that once, while she was at Conyers' home, he "came out of the bathroom completely naked."

After initially defending Conyers as an "icon," House Minority Leader Nancy Pelosi, D-Calif., called for Conyers to resign. Her call for his resignation, however, came 50 years too late.

For what has Conyers, a co-founder of the Congressional Black Caucus, achieved in his over half-century of service? Every two years since 1989, Conyers has introduced a bill for reparations for slavery. It has never gotten out of committee.

This blacks-are-owed-something-because-of-slavery mindset is dangerous and counterproductive. It is this mindset that is the basis for "affirmative action," or race-based preferences.

While "affirmative action" to achieve "diversity" is now a staple on college campuses, some warned about its unintended negative consequences. Archie Epps was one. He served as one of Harvard's first black deans. He criticized Harvard for admitting unqualified black students, and warned the school as early as the late '60s about the perils of admitting scholastically unqualified students to achieve "diversity." Epps predicted that lowered standards for incoming black students would lead to a higher dropout rate, precisely what has happened.

Similarly, Judge Macklin Fleming, a former Yale graduate, wrote a letter in 1969 warning the dean of Yale Law School about its new "quota" policy, which guaranteed that 10 percent of each entering class would be composed of black students. Fleming predicted that "minority groups" that outperform relative to blacks, such as Asian-Americans, would be penalized in favor of lesser-qualified minorities. He predicted that those admitted with lower standards would struggle academically. The students, Fleming predicted, would make demands for watered-down courses or would accuse "racist" professors of giving them poor grades. All of this, he argued, would create a supposition that minorities are not as competent as non-minorities. Their degrees would be viewed with suspicion.

Conyers supports race-based preferences. Yet in 2000, The Detroit News evaluated the affirmative action programs of seven colleges and universities in Michigan. They reported: "Among black students who were freshmen in 1994, just 40 percent got their diplomas after six years, compared to 61 percent of white students and 74 percent of Asians. ... Universities knowingly admit students who have a high chance of failing. ... The 10 years' worth of data analyzed by The News shows that the more selective a university is in choosing its students, the more likely its students are to graduate."

One history professor even said: "We're throwing them out after taking their money and they're getting nothing out of it. We're mugging (the majority) of them, taking their money, taking their dignity. I feel like I am participating in a vast criminal conspiracy."

Conyers opposes school vouchers, which would allow the money for education to follow the student rather than the other way around. In Detroit, the average urban high school student reads several grades below grade level. Urban parents want vouchers so they can send their child to a private or parochial school, and not to the underperforming public school chosen by government.

Conyers opposes the privatization of Social Security. The libertarian think tank CATO Institute calculates that because blacks die at a younger age, there is a net transfer of about $10,000 from black workers to non-black workers.

Conyers does not understand the connection between the welfare state and the demise of the nuclear black family. In 1965, 25 percent of black babies were born to unmarried mothers. Fifty years later, and over $22 trillion spent on the "War on Poverty," and now 72 percent of black kids are born out of wedlock.

Conyers' indifference about open borders allows unskilled illegal workers to compete for urban jobs and puts downward pressure on wages.

It is long past time for Conyers to pack up his race cards and call it a career.

Trump's 'Abysmal' Poll Numbers? What About Those of Merkel, Macron, May and Trudeau?

December 14, 2017

About a year into President Donald Trump's first term, the jury for much of the country and for most of the major media has returned its verdict: Trump is a failure. Trump is incompetent. Trump cannot lead. Trump has no legislative victories. Even former President Jimmy Carter said he had never seen a president so maligned in the media. Meanwhile former President Barack Obama all but compared Trump to Hitler.

Trump endures a nightly beating from the cast of late-night comedians who take turns calling Trump racist, sexist, dumb, inarticulate, overweight, overwrought and, of course, clueless. His reported consumption of 12 Diet Cokes per day provided material for the comics' writers. Nothing seems to be off limits, not even first lady Melania's choice of White House Christmas decor.

Based on the beating Trump endures daily from a hostile "news" media, coupled with the nightly drubbing at the hands of Stephen Colbert, Jimmy Fallon, Jimmy Kimmel et al, one could reasonably assume that Trump's approval ratings must be among the worst any leader could have. Trump got pounded by much of the left for his decision to move the American embassy in Israel from Tel Aviv to Jerusalem. Never mind every president since 1995 has promised to do so.

Trump got hammered for backing Judge Roy Moore in the Alabama Senate race. Trump first backed Moore's Republican primary opponent. When Moore won, Trumped switched his support to him. But when several allegations came out about Moore's alleged sexual misconduct, Trump called on him to drop out "if the allegations are true." The Republican National Committee pulled its endorsement and funding. Trump then did a 180, presumably fearing the loss of a Republican Senate vote in a chamber that is only 52-48 Republican versus Democrat.

Democrats used the allegations against Moore to remind voters of the "Access Hollywood" tape in which Trump made crude remarks about women and fame.

When the Rasmussen poll put Trump's approval rating at 46 percent a month ago, comedian Jimmy Fallon quipped: "Did you see this? Trump just went on Twitter and bragged about a poll showing that he has a 46 percent approval rating. Really? That's like posting a math quiz on the fridge where you got a D-plus."

But how many Trump haters know that his "D-plus" is still better than the grades of leaders of other important countries?

Take Germany's internationally respected Chancellor Angela Merkel, the leader of her party since 2000 and the head of the federal government since 2005. According to The Times of London, the approval number for her and her party just three weeks ago was an all-time low of 29.2 percent: "Angela Merkel's poll ratings fell to an all-time low yesterday after the breakdown of talks on forming a coalition government as the German president, Frank-Walter Steinmeier, stepped up efforts to avoid new elections."

How about France's President Emmanuel Macron? According to the U.K.'s Daily Express headline in October, "Emmanuel Macron Loses France's Trust: Poll Shows Majority Questioned Have No Faith in Him." The Express reported: "The majority of French people — 54 per cent — 'do not trust the head of state to fix the country's social and economic problems,' according to the Elabe poll for Radio Classique and Les Echos. ... His current approval ratings, however, pale in comparison to his high post-election ratings, when some 60 per cent of French voters expressed satisfaction with their new leader." Recall the zeal with which some in the U.S. media greeted Macron's election. Time magazine reported: "An untested whizkid has shot to power as President of France in his very first election campaign, crumpling older, hard-bitten veterans in his wake. ... Aged just 39, Macron is France's youngest leader since the famed French emperor Napoleon Bonaparte, who took power at age 35."

Then there's Britain's Prime Minister Theresa May. The Telegraph reported last month on a poll by ORB International: "It shows that two in three people disapprove of the way the Brexit negotiations are being handled. ... Some 44 per cent of the public backed her at the start of June, but after she lost the Conservatives' parliamentary majority in a snap election that she called, the figure dropped to 34 per cent. It is now just 26 per cent."

Finally, look at the poll numbers of Canada's Justin Trudeau. According to Bloomberg Businessweek, his numbers are down significantly from when he was elected: "Two years into Trudeau's first term, a polling aggregator run by the Canadian Broadcasting Corp. shows his support at 37.9 percent, down eight points from a year ago — still strong in Canada's three-party system."

Yes, Trump's numbers are low — for now. But other leaders on the world stage are doing worse, in some instances far worse. So before much of the country and the media write Trump off as a failure, how about we try just a little perspective?

Suppose President Barack Obama Spent Year 1 Battling 'Collusion'?

December 21, 2017

Imagine how Democrats, the media, academia and Hollywood would have reacted had the newly elected President Barack Obama, America's first black president, spent the first year of his presidency with his campaign and transition teams under investigation for "collusion" to steal the election.

Imagine if, from the very moment Obama won the election, Republicans reminded the country that Sen. Obama campaigned against what he considered President George W. Bush's dark, hawkish vision of foreign policy. And that Obama wanted to curry favor with Russia, whose assistance Obama wanted to secure the Iran nuke deal his administration so desperately wanted.

Imagine Obama supporters' reaction had Republicans, immediately after Obama's election, pushed the following narrative. Russia wanted Obama to win so Vladimir Putin could get him to reverse the Poland and Czech Republic defense deals that Russia strongly opposed. Obama, as president, delivered. (In fact, one of President Obama's first major foreign policy decisions reversed the missile defense deals Bush 43 negotiated with Poland and the Czech Republic.) So, say the Republicans, Obama was Russia's guy. Imagine the explosion in this country had Bush's top intelligence official called the newly elected Obama a Russian "asset" who does Putin's bidding, just as former National Intelligence Director James Clapper recently described President Donald Trump.

Imagine that Republicans claimed Obama did not earn the presidency: He stole it, used an ancient Jedi mind trick to sucker the American people into walking into that booth and punching that ballot for America's first black president.

Imagine if cable news televised hearing after hearing where Republicans aggressively questioned Obama officials about "collusion" with the Russians to win the election. Sen. Diane Feinstein, D-Calif., often a voice of reason in her party, admitted that in the Trump investigations, so far, she sees no evidence of collusion, let alone illegal collusion. What would she have said if the target were Obama rather than Trump?

Imagine that "after all this time and expense" spent on an Obama collusion investigation, Democrats argue that investigators found no evidence of collusion, but then the investigation shifts. The probe goes from whether Obama worked with Putin to win the election to whether anyone lied to investigators during the investigation — no matter the fact the "lies" had nothing to do with whether illegal collusion occurred.

Imagine how Obama supporters would react to Republicans who first attributed Obama's win to illegal collusion, but then began saying, "It's not the crime; it's the cover-up," or "It's the obstruction of justice." Even more strident Republicans would likely note that the Communist Party USA no longer runs its own candidates for president but now supports Democrats, as they did Obama.

In fact, we really don't have to imagine. There is a parallel.

Recall how quickly Obama defenders cried racism when Republicans simply expressed policy differences. Actor Morgan Freeman all but called Senate GOP leader Mitch McConnell, R-Ky., "racist" for, in effect, saying that America will be better off if he works to make Obama a "one-term president." Obama supporters still cite the "you lie" outburst from Rep. Joe Wilson, R-S.C., as a top exhibit for the "racist" disrespect supposedly accorded the first black president by Republicans. Former President Jimmy Carter even blamed racism for the vociferous opposition to Obamacare, as if there hadn't been intense opposition against Hillarycare 15 years earlier.

Editorials in virtually every major newspaper would blast an investigation of Obama. Most would call it racially motivated. An avalanche of angry editorials and opinion pieces would attack the "subversive effort to overturn this historic election." Imagine the outcry from editorials, pundits, former officials, college professors, actors and members of the clergy, demanding to know whether Republicans would go after a white male president with the kind of vengeance as they had this black one, whose very place of birth, they'd say, had been questioned by "birther" Republicans.

Cable TV commentators on CNN and MSNBC would have predicted, and prepared to cover, riots in the streets should Obama be impeached. Black Lives Matter leaders would encourage people to "take to the streets." Leaders would shout, "They can't even define 'collusion.'" "When did trying to get dirt on your opponent become a crime?" "This is nothing more than an attempt by white racists to undo an election because they still cannot believe a black man won." And on and on.

Every House and Senate Democrat would gather on the steps of the Capital to show solidarity, denounce the Obama probe and demand the firings of investigators who, in their view, "have shown bias." Civil rights leaders would call it "political lynching" by a party that wants "to bring back Jim Crow, turn back the clock on civil rights and suppress the black vote." Leaders would warn of an impending "civil war" if the probe continued.

And *then*, it would get ugly.

Why is Maxine Waters Silent on The Terrorist Drug-Dealing Probe That Obama Shut Down?

December 28, 2017

Rep. Maxine Waters, D-Calif., once falsely accused President Ronald Reagan's CIA of all but causing urban cocaine dealing in the '80s. She claimed that Reagan, by working with Nicaraguan drug dealers to defeat the communists running that country, colluded with them to created the urban drug epidemic. Never mind that The New York Times, The Washington Post and the Los Angeles Times all debunked Waters' claim.

At a town hall meeting about these allegations, Waters shouted, "If I never do anything else in this career as a member of Congress, I'm gonna make somebody pay for what they've done to my community and to my people!" Yet as to "Politico's" bombshell claim that in order to negotiate a nuclear deal with Iran, President Barack Obama allowed an Iran-funded Hezbollah terrorist/drug-dealing mastermind who worked for Russian President Putin to continue to operate. Yet Waters, who calls for President Donald Trump's impeachment, has said absolutely nothing.

How desperate was Obama to negotiate a nuclear deal with Iran?

In his zeal not to offend Iran so he could complete the deal, Obama halted a George W. Bush administration investigation of drug and human trafficking by the Iran-funded terror group Hezbollah. According to "Politico," the Obama administration angered investigators by interfering with and shutting down a well-funded and resourced Drug Enforcement Agency probe known as Project Cassandra.

In "The Secret Backstory of How Obama Let Hezbollah Off the Hook," Politico senior investigator Josh Meyer wrote about the investigation the government called "Project Cassandra" and Ali Fayad, a Hezbollah operative suspected of, among other things, of using profits from drug-dealing to finance terror operations and to move weapons to Syria.

Meyer writes: "When Project Cassandra leaders sought approval for some significant investigations, prosecutions, arrests and financial sanctions, officials at the Justice and Treasury departments delayed, hindered or rejected their requests.

"The Justice Department declined requests by Project Cassandra and other authorities to file criminal charges against major players such as Hezbollah's high-profile envoy to Iran, a Lebanese bank that allegedly laundered billions in alleged drug profits, and a central player in a U.S.-based cell of the Iranian paramilitary Quds force. And the State Department rejected requests to lure high-value targets to countries where they could be arrested. ...

"Lebanese arms dealer Ali Fayad, a suspected top Hezbollah operative whom agents believed reported to Russian President Vladimir Putin as a key supplier of weapons to Syria and Iraq, was arrested in Prague in the spring of 2014. But for the nearly two years Fayad was in custody, top Obama administration officials declined to apply serious pressure on the Czech government to extradite him to the United States, even as Putin was lobbying aggressively against it.

"Fayad, who had been indicted in U.S. courts on charges of planning the murders of U.S. government employees, attempting to provide material support to a terrorist organization and attempting to acquire, transfer and use anti-aircraft missiles, was ultimately sent to Beirut. He is now believed by U.S. officials to be back in business, and helping to arm militants in Syria and elsewhere with Russian heavy weapons.

"Project Cassandra members say administration officials also blocked or undermined their efforts to go after other top Hezbollah operatives including one ... of the world's biggest cocaine traffickers, including to the U.S., as well as a major supplier of conventional and chemical weapons for use by Syrian President Bashar Assad against his people."

Recall that last year, The New York Times reported that Obama's point man on the Iran Deal, deputy national security adviser Ben Rhodes, pushed the Iran Deal by peddling a phony narrative that Iran's "moderate" ayatollahs were battling the "hard-liners." This nuclear deal to supposedly halt Iran's march toward acquiring a nuclear bomb, Rhodes argued, and would strengthen the hand of the alleged moderates.

Among those who questioned the logic of this deal was none other than Obama's first secretary of Defense, Robert Gates, who called it a "hope" that he considered "unrealistic." Gates, who left the administration before the Obama completed the deal, said, "I think that the pursuit of the agreement is based on the president's hope that over a 10-year period with the sanctions being lifted that ... they will abandon their ideology, their theology, their revolutionary principles, their meddling in various parts of the region. And, frankly, I believe that's very unrealistic."

All of this is jaw-dropping. Equally incredible is the major media indifference to this big story. In the days following Politico's story, Fox News, the Wall Street Journal and the New York Post covered the story — but it was ignored by practically every other cable news and newspaper outlet. The story did not make the cut for the nightly newscasts of NBC, ABC and CBS, which still have a combined 20 million daily viewers.

Silent, too, was Congresswoman Waters. How many of these drugs ended up in the streets of America's cities?

About the Author

A "firebrand libertarian" according to Daily Variety, best-selling author, radio and TV talk show host Larry Elder has a take-no-prisoners style, using such old-fashioned things as evidence and logic. Larry shines the bright light of reasoned analysis on many of the myths and hypocrisies apparent in our system of government, our society, and the media itself. He slays dragons and topples sacred cows using facts, common sense and a ready wit.

Larry hosted, for 15 years, the longest-running afternoon drive-time radio show in Los Angeles, beginning in March 1994. "The Larry Elder Show," a top-rated daily program from 3 p.m. to 7 p.m. on KABC 790, became a nationally syndicated daily talk show for ABC Radio Networks on Aug. 12, 2002. Now Larry is seeking airwave dominance over the morning hours, broadcasting from KABC from 9 a.m. until noon. Known to his listeners as the "Sage From South Central," Larry sizzles on the airwaves with his thoughtful insight on the day's most provocative issues, to the delight, consternation and entertainment of his listeners.

In his best-selling book "The 10 Things You Can't Say in America," Larry skewers the crippling myths that dominate the public agenda. Larry punctures all pretension, trashes accepted "wisdom" and puts everyone on notice that the status quo must be shaken up. In his second book, "Showdown: Confronting Bias, Lies and the Special Interests That Divide America," Larry again takes on the Nanny State, "victicrats" and the politically correct. His latest book, "What's Race Got to Do with It? Why it's Time to Stop the Stupidest Argument in America," is being praised as an important, groundbreaking must-read for the future of race relations in America. Elder also writes a nationally syndicated newspaper column, distributed through Creators Syndicate.

Larry was also host of the television shows "Moral Court" and "The Larry Elder Show." Larry created, directed and produced his first film, "Michael & Me," a documentary that examines the use of guns in America.

BAD NEWS FOR RACE HUSTLERS
is also available as an e-book
for Kindle, Amazon Fire, iPad, Nook and
Android e-readers. Visit
creatorspublishing.com to learn more.

∘ ∘ ∘

CREATORS PUBLISHING

We publish books.
We find compelling storytellers and
help them craft their narrative,
distributing their novels and collections
worldwide.

∘ ∘ ∘

CPSIA information can be obtained
at www.ICGtesting.com
Printed in the USA
LVHW052259260619
622502LV00002B/138/P